COPY

YOUR WAY TO

SUCCESS

Standing on the Shoulders of Giants

COREY PETERSON

FOUNDER OF KAHUNA WEALTH BUILDERS

DEDICATION

Dad, you have always been a greek god in my eyes and my hero. So many times, I remember you leaving early for work as a roofer, to come home late, but you never seemed tired. You mustered up the strength to play full-out with me and my other brothers and sisters. We all wanted to be by your side and hear your jolly laugh and see the brightness in your eyes.

You taught me the value of hard work and doing your best. You taught me right from wrong, and how to stand up for yourself and be a man.

Although you have a few more miles, my kids want to be around to hear your laugh and see that twinkle in your eyes too.

I dedicate this book to you. I am your son. Mighty Mighty Petersons forever.

TABLE OF CONTENTS

INTRODUCTION

FIRST AND FOREMOST, I want to thank you for taking the time to come on this journey with me as I guide you through what I have learned since 2005 when I first started my company, Kahuna Investments, and became a multimillionaire through real estate investments.

This book builds upon three very simple ideas:

- You don't have to create something new to become wildly successful.

- You have a mission in your heart—a deep desire to be great, and the courage to learn what you don't know in order to make a difference.

- By following others who have paved the path, you can shortcut your way to success and have the two things people crave most: time and money.

If you're like most people, at some point, you've dreamed or envisioned becoming your own boss. You start out full of excitement and with the attitude that you will work long hours and do whatever it takes to be successful as an entrepreneur. That honeymoon period vanishes quickly and you come to realize that you have a real business that involves many moving parts. In the beginning, it's typically one person performing all the roles. Most people are not prepared to wear so many hats in a new business, and the struggle is real.

Meanwhile, other companies in the same businesses are doing fine. They are making great income by running successful systems that were more than likely copied off someone who is already thriving, providing them with a shorter runway to success.

What if you could peek inside their business and get a front-row view of everything they did to become successful in the first place? Would that be of great value to you? Better yet, what if you could sit down with the owner, have lunch with him, and pick his brain? Do you think you would learn something?

Here's what I know. The world is changing faster than ever. We are in the Informational Age. This shift started with the computer and internet. Believe it or not, we're still in the virgin years.

Yet, ironically, people are settling. Instead of tapping into all of the resources readily available at their fingertips, people are settling for that secure job. You know the one—just over broke, that pays just enough to get by, but not enough to *live.*

We've tricked ourselves into believing it's worth it. What happened to us? When did we let go of our passion and dreams? I think we reprogram ourselves over time. Society tells us to play it safe, go to school, get your degree, and find that good job. That is the standard success route most of us grew up with. It's the path most of our parents laid out for us.

But, this safe route often drains us and puts us in zombie mode. We start each day the same way, tackling the same problems and becoming consumed by a passionless existence controlled by a safe promise of income. Yet, we all know, no job is ever safe. People get laid off every day, and the old adage of working for the same company for thirty years and collecting a pension has long left the train station.

Moreover, the rich keep getting richer, and the middle class is becoming the lower middle class. In fact, it nearly takes two incomes just to make ends meet.

As a result of both parents working, we are busy, busy, busy, and at times, we forget to look up and see what's happening to us. Our lives become a routine, much like the movie with Bill Murray, *Groundhog's Day* where we go on doing the same thing over and over again. Before we know it, our light or spirit, which once used to be bright and full of ambition, is now a dim, hopeless mess.

In addition to settling, business owners get tired and stressed out by not fully understanding the work and systems required. Instead of spending quality time working "ON the business," they choose to put on all the hats and work knee-deep "IN the business," resulting in doing many small jobs they may not be qualified for. Yet, they wonder why they're not making money. They end up hating the business and feel like it's a big ball and chain they carry around for life. I know so many entrepreneurs who have felt this way at one time or another.

What if you could set up a business part-time and start learning the systems needed to be successful? What if you could stick one foot in and still keep that stable job while working on your own company? Maybe working five to fifteen hours a week instead of sixty plus?

There's something uniquely different that sets awesome businesses apart from the mediocre companies. The ones really crushing it consider themselves experts and have expert systems and processes. You see, experts, no matter what the field, tend to make more money than generalists.

Let that sink in for a moment.

Having said all this, there is hope for you and all who dare to dream again. I want to take you on my journey of how I became a multimillionaire by copying others. I want to show you how you can, too. You can do this while still having the secure job while you transition. I have made my money in real estate, but don't be fooled, you can use my examples and apply them to any industry. All you have to be is curious, hungry, and ready for a change.

This is not a hype book. This is a book about struggle, courage, passion, self-doubt, depression, pity, achievement, triumph, leadership, pain, and ultimately, success.

This book is about the life we lead and the life we want. I hope to, at the very least, wake you up from your sleep and awaken the giant within you. We all have gifts, but many of us never use them to our full potential.

For me, things were not always easy. I grew up

in a small farm town in Crider, MO and barely made it out of high school.

This farm boy will never forget where he started.

I didn't get the download from the mothership or my life's mission until I was 32 years old. I started in real estate with no money and no credit, yet in twelve short years have become a multimillionaire.

I did all this by following others. I did not go rogue and do it all by myself. I took ideas and systems from others, made them mine, and went to work.

I'm going to show you step-by-step how I started my journey and ultimately became successful. I challenge you to follow me.

You can start now by subscribing to my podcast,

Multi-Family Legacy Podcast on iTunes. If you really want some great free training, text the word "Dream" to 480-500-1127, and let me unlock some real estate ideas. You don't have to choose real estate as the industry you want to copy. My examples can transfer to any business, but once you see how I've done it, you may want to stick around.

I know you can copy your way to success in real estate investing and make millions of dollars in it. I mean, if a guy who is deaf in his right ear, talks out of one side of his mouth, is only 5'9," and barely made it out of high school can do it, I promise you, you can kill it. So, stick around and read this thing because once I'm done with you, you will be enlightened, engaged, and ready to make a difference.

MY FIRST FLIP...
WAS A FLOP

I'D LOVE TO SAY I was successful right out of the gate, but that isn't the case. I tried it on my own, thought I could zig and zag my way through to a big check, but I had forgotten a strategy that had worked my entire life: copying.

As you read on, you'll realize I've been copying people who are better than me since grade school. While it might have been frowned upon back then, it worked for me.

The strategy was so ingrained in me, I didn't even realize I was doing it. I'd watch baseball with my dad and critique my favorite player's form, then try my hardest to replicate it in the backyard. I'd watch the other kids on the way home and find the shortcuts that allowed me to cut through the creek and make it home ten minutes quicker.

But when it came to real estate investing, I did it all wrong in the beginning. I read any book on real estate I could find. I scoured the Barnes and Noble shelves searching for the answers and knowledge I needed to be successful. Some of the techniques seemed very old-school, but I didn't know where else to turn. This was my only guidance and I didn't take advantage like I should have. I was young and dumb.

In the very beginning, I made a critical, costly mistake. I tried to do it on my own, without any help, and I failed in a huge way.

You see, I got a few deals under my belt, but had virtually no money coming in, and I was out of options. I had no idea how to move further. Copying my way to success had been my strength since I was a kid, and I did not implement this strategy while starting out. If I could tell my young self just one thing, it would be to watch other successful real estate investors from the beginning and do exactly what they do.

Unsure of myself, with no one to turn to, I put my real estate dreams on hold and told myself I needed to make good income to start doing deals again.

I only wish I had someone to talk to at this point in my life or a book I could relate my situation to. I longed for a book that showed me the journey of becoming a real estate investor through the tough times in the beginning, to the growing pains of success. The reason I wrote this book is to guide you on the correct path without making the mistakes that I did. Most books talk about how great it is, but they forget to mention the struggle and how to get out of it.

My point is, I've made about every mistake in this business you can make. Because I've been on a journey for over fourteen years, I have fourteen years of mistakes to share and help guide you so you won't make the same mistakes I did.

Furthermore, if you had a choice of who to learn from, would you want someone who has been there, done that, or someone who has been there, done that, and is still doing it?

I hope you'd opt for the latter. Doing it now is a big, big thing. Always be a skeptic of where the information is coming from and whether it is relevant now. If they were successful five years ago, but haven't done a deal this year, do you think they know the most current strategies out there?

<u>Opportunities Are Everywhere</u>

Whether you know it or not, the economy is moving and opportunities are everywhere. In the Great Recession that hit in 2007-2008, a lot of fortunes became eroded, but a down economy also breeds millionaires overnight. Look at the greats, like Robert Allen, Robert Kiyosaki, and Donald Trump. Their wealth and holdings grew tenfold as those economies came out of the ashes. Our last downturn will go down in history as the second biggest next to the Great Depression. This also means a longer and more sustainable upside, and this is why the time could not be better to invest in real estate, specifically cash-flowing apartment complexes.

Not only do I believe the timing couldn't be better, but a lot of things have also changed in the marketplace, which is exciting and rewarding. For instance, let's talk about technology.

With technology, you aren't stuck investing in your backyard anymore because information about other markets is at your fingertips. You can find out how other cities' job creation is doing. You can see if more people are moving in than moving out, you can research anything you can think of. It's as easy as opening up your laptop and typing it into Google.

This easy access to important data helps you to make more informed decisions when looking into new markets and new opportunities to invest outside of the market you live in. What's even better is that most people have access to info via the web, but not many truly capitalize on this.

This makes becoming an expert much easier than you think.

There are software programs out there that make crunching numbers and analyzing deals so much easier and efficient. You can get mine at **www.KahunaCashflowCalculator.com**. In fact, once you get a good system of deal analysis and deal flow coming into your business, you can train virtual assistants who live in other countries to do most of the heavy lifting for you. They can screen deals, run comps, and really do an overall workup of the local economy. They can do it at a rate per hour no one here in the USA would ever do. With the internet, you can outsource and get things done without having to set aside large amounts of capital.

Now, I've told you a lot of the good things going on in our economy and why it's really exciting. But there is a dark side or underbelly to watch out for as well. Today more than ever, the rich are getting richer, and the poor are getting poorer. Which side will you fall on as the middle class erodes?

Companies are consolidating at rapid speed. Just like I mentioned above, it makes financial sense to hire assistants from other countries who are loyal, cheap, and easy to train on routine tasks. Without them, entrepreneurs wouldn't be able to rise to success as quickly because of having to pay three-to-six times the hourly rate for a US based employee compared to someone overseas.

Don't get stuck in the middle where jobs are being replaced with technology or outsourcing. The time to put your foot in the entrepreneur stage is more important now than ever.

You need to be the job creator, not the job taker.

Now that I've shown you the good, the bad, and the ugly, let's talk about who wins and who loses in the Informational Age when it comes to real estate and business in general.

The winners are going to be the ones who are leveraging technology and collaborating with other successful people in their industry. Have an abundance mindset. Find other like-minded people. Share ideas and strategies with them so that everyone comes out a winner.

Big Idea:

There's power in people coming together to share their best practices and ideas.

- *Surround yourself with people in your industry who are better than you.*

- *Be curious. Find out exactly what they are doing, the systems they are using, marketing, processes, people, etc.*

- *Give your best ideas. Be a big giver. You will never regret it.*

The people who are unwilling to change will lose. Change is a constant in life, but in the Informational Age, it happens a lot faster than it used to. Think about it. If you work in technology, the way things were done five years ago, or even one year ago, do not work the same today.

Those businesses or individuals who do not keep up with the times end up in the business graveyard. Take Blockbuster for example. My family looked forward to Friday movie nights running to Blockbuster and hoping they still had a copy of the latest release before they sold out for the weekend. Blockbuster had the movie rental market figured out, and they were thriving until a little company called Netflix came along and Blockbuster didn't change with the times.

Think of all the customers Blockbuster had. If they would have been willing to change its model and used the customer base they already had, things could have been very different. My point is this: Things will continue to change, and you will not want to be wondering what is happening. You want to be ahead of the curve.

So how do you stay ahead of the curve? In my own life, although I don't have a college degree, I have been on a relentless journey for knowledge and information when it comes to real estate. I've read countless books and listened to lots of audio tapes. I've been to one too many seminars trying to glean pearls of wisdom. I find that this one constant in my life is what puts me over the competition. It's sad, but I see so many college graduates get a diploma and consider their education done. Except, some of the most important things you'll learn will be after you're done with school and in the real world.

For me, the journey is the reward, and learning new things is part of the process.

But, it wasn't easy.

My biggest leaps came when I learned from a true mentor who showed me how to use a technique that was working in that particular market cycle. So, hold on and pay attention as we continue to unpack the mystery of how to unlock the game of real estate by following others and copying what works so you can win—and win big.

First, let me give you a little more background on my story and my struggles so you may see for yourself you can do this.

PICKING ROCK

WHEN I WAS IN third grade going into fourth, my life became starkly different. I was living in Las Vegas, Nevada. I considered myself to be a city kid. I rode my bike to school every day, had lots of friends in my neighborhood, and never spent much time inside.

My father was a journeyman roofer, and something was going on at his work. The union was starting to get greedy. They wanted more money than employers could pay, and it was only a matter of time before the union's back became crushed against the wall. So, we packed up the U-Haul and headed to West Plains, Missouri, where my grandma and grandpa lived. My dad was going to start his own business.

It didn't take Dad long to find a 180-acre farm in Crider, Missouri, thirty minutes from what we would consider a town. As for Crider, it had one store with two gas pumps ran by a man named Big John. I was plucked out of the city and given a shovel on a farm, essentially. I hated that first summer because of the drastic change to country livin', but as I look back, the wilderness family move, taking a city kid and putting him in the country, was the best gift my parents could have ever given me.

__FARM LIFE__

Farm life is not easy. My dad had a roofing company in the city, but I think his passion was farming or running cattle. His passion for me and my two brothers was to make us into men by showing us how to work.

We call that picking rock.

Now, country people know what picking rock means. It means you plow a field, then you take a farm truck or tractor and walk behind it all day long picking up stupid rocks from the soil and putting them into a truck bed.

On a 180-acre field, you can do this for at least a week, sometimes longer. We picked rock in the middle of summer in ninety-five-degree weather with ninety percent humidity. It is in these times you find out what you're made of. Dad expected this job to get done, so we didn't have a choice. My father did not run a democracy in our household. There were no debates. Dad had a dictatorship, and he called all the shots. His word was the law. So, unless we wanted a beating, we picked rock.

Did I mention that before you ever get to put a hand on a twenty-pound rock, you got to bale and buck fifty-pound hay bales?

You have never lived until you have baled hay. You can't bale hay unless you are covered from head to toe—jeans, a T-shirt, some type of flannel shirt, work boots, and gloves. And guess what? It's still the middle of summer—ninety-five degrees; ninety percent humidity.

Now, those are the summer chores that always have to get done. I haven't touched on the winter chores. Once you get all that hay in the barn, you then take it out every week and load a pickup and take it out into a field to feed your cattle. Not to mention when you get bundled up from head to toe and head out to the ponds with an ax in hand to break the ice so your cattle can have a drink of water. You get to go every day to make sure that ice hasn't formed.

Finally, we come to my favorite daily chore, bottle feeding calves. My dad had built special chutes to where we could feed eight to ten calves every morning. My younger brothers, older sister, and I were each responsible for feeding two calves in rain, sleet, snow, ice, extreme heat. No matter what, they had to get fed. We always did this before we got on the bus.

It was always a very bad day if you did not wake up early enough and put your good shoes on instead of your cow boots to feed the calves. This meant on the hour bus ride to school no one wanted to sit by you because you smelled like you had stepped into something and no one liked the smell of it. The smell of cow poop will always haunt me.

So why do I share this way of farm life?

I want to show you how my father taught me the value of hard work. He taught me the discipline of doing things right and being able to put in an honest day's work. My dad taught me always to do my best. If you did your best, you could always hold your head up high.

Better yet, you would always be able to look another man in the eye. But looking back, what my father was teaching me was something else entirely.

Don't own a farm unless you love this type of work or can pay someone else to do it.

Big Idea:

Hard work is needed to get things done.

I want to stress that it takes work to get things done. But it doesn't have to be just your work, and it does not have to be hard. The most successful people are in motion, not sitting on the sidelines.

Farm life taught me a work ethic, but it also taught me how to dream big. On the 180-acre farm, we had a very big playground. My closest neighbor was two miles away on a dirt road. To keep yourself entertained, you had to have an imagination. I have always been a big dreamer. I'd climb trees out in the woods and hang up there daydreaming of what I wanted to do with my life.

There were times I was a professional baseball player, and I'd imagine myself in a game up to bat and how I'd hit the grand slam. I would imagine how it would feel, hearing the crack of the ball coming off my wooden bat. I'd watch the ball take off in flight. I'd hear the crowd roar to life and man, it was all very real to me. In those early years of my life, I never reined in my imagination. I fed it and fed it daily. I allowed myself to dream without any restrictions.

It's amazing what you can think of when you don't put limits on what is possible.

When my brother and I would saddle up our Fox Trotter horses and go horseback riding to Devils Backbone in the Mark Twain National Forest, I'd imagine I was the Lone Ranger, and my job was to protect my brothers. I may not have had a six-shooter, but my .22 rifle was up on the saddle, and I knew how to use it. My brothers and I would spend hours upon hours playing make-believe in those woods and then do it all over again the next day. We had a passion for it, and we felt alive.

Big Idea:

Dream big. Dream often. Dream like a child.

Take time right now and think about your biggest, wildest dreams. What did it feel like to feel optimistic about life? How did <u>you</u> dream? How did you view what you could achieve?

I believe a lot of people reading this book right now were like me back then. You used to dream amazingly big. You had a vision you used to believe you could achieve and someone, somewhere along the way, clouded that vision. In that state of mind, you began to self-doubt. Ultimately, you gave up or put that dream on standby. A child's mind is a very precious thing, and at that point in my life, I felt invincible. Nothing could prepare me for what was coming.

Life was about to come at me like a pitcher throwing hard, nasty heat, and I was going to have trouble with the curve.

MY MIKE TYSON KNOCKOUT

I N SEVENTH GRADE, my life was shattered, and my beliefs were rocked to the core. I wanted to be a professional baseball player. My father, before his roofing days, had achieved it as a catcher for the Cleveland Indians AA team, and I wanted to follow in his footsteps.

It was constantly on my mind and I was determined. My imagination had grown to be so vivid while out in the country, and it was my safe haven.

When out on the farm, I would pick up rocks and imagine I was playing catcher with the runner on first base trying to steal second. I could see it in his eyes as he slowed, trying to increase his leadoff. You could feel the nervousness and knew he was go-

ing to run. I called for a fastball, high and outside, and set myself up to quickly catch the ball using two hands and transfer the ball to my throwing hand. I instantly lined up the laces of the ball, so when I threw it, all four laces cut through the air, allowing the ball to rise and maximize its distance.

I had to be quick and accurate. I would launch my rock right at a wooden post that held miles of barbed wire fence. I knew I had thrown him out when I heard a loud clunk from the rock bouncing off the post.

When that happened, I would look down at the shortstop. He would kick a little dirt my way letting me know "good throw" and "atta boy." It was a sign of respect. The crowd would yell, and the re-play on the TV screens showed the speed and ac-curacy of my throw. I would play this out in multiple scenarios a million times a day. Baseball wasn't just a passion—it was my mission.

When you're young, you believe you can do anything, and my mind was constantly at work. It was how I coped with not having friends who could easily come over. My mind was my playground, and I never reeled it in.

One day in school, our teacher was having a de-bate and asked us what we wanted to be when we grew up. At first, I was reluctant to raise my hand for fear of being judged, but I had been keeping this inside for so long, I was finally ready to share it with the world—I was ready to show the world my dreams.

My teacher called upon me, and I proudly walked to the front of the class and summoned all my strength as I boldly proclaimed, "I am going to become a professional baseball player." I did it! I had finally said it, and boy did it feel good. The secret I had been carrying with me for six years was finally out, and I was so proud of myself and filled with excitement.

What came next was like Mike Tyson's punchout . . .

The teacher looked me dead in the eyes and, without remorse, told the class, based upon the odds, I would never achieve it—If he were taking odds in Vegas, he would bet against me.

Everyone started to laugh, and I just sat there in the front of the class, not sure how to respond. Something happened inside that I couldn't explain. My mind was racing as I stumbled back to my desk, and the questions started in. What if he's right? Could he really know? What were the odds of becoming a professional? Am I good enough? I wanted to scream out I was going to do it—I was going to become a professional—yet it seemed cloudy now.

That vision, which used to be crystal clear, became foggy and confusing. This was all because of one man's words. As I looked around the room, it seemed all my classmates believed him as well.

How could they fall for this?

How could they not see how I had dreamed about this since I was seven years old?

Why didn't they realize what they were doing was tearing my heart apart?

All I had ever wanted was to be like my dad. I wanted to make him proud and go farther than he did. While I felt the need to scream out, I instead dropped my head as the doubt bombarded me. Maybe I wasn't good enough. Maybe I was living a pipedream.

That day rocked me to the core. The more I looked around, the more I heard what people were telling me.

No.

You can't.

You're not good enough.

And I started to believe they were right.

Isn't this what happens to us? When we want to try something new or reach for something big, someone comes along and tells us the forty ways we'll fail. Instead of encouraging, they tear you down. It's usually the ones closest to you—your family, friends, and loved ones.

It took me years to build up my confidence again. I went on a mission of feeling like I had to prove my worth. I became a Tommy Topper. If you had a story about something you did, I had a better one—always one-upping, always needing to be the best. Then, one day, it all clicked—I had matured and began to understand what was happening. People say things they do not mean or even understand.

The fact is, the response my teacher gave me is a very normal response, and it should be expected. You see, when people dream big and fail, your family, friends, and loved ones see the pain. That pain is what people think of when you tell them about your new dream and goal. They automatically assume the worst can and will happen because they want to protect you and don't like seeing you in pain. This is the mindset your family, friends, and loved ones use when they are forming their opinion. It's always conservative. Truthfully, you are counting on them to reel you in. People always flock to safety. But, guess what, we are never safe.

TAKING THE POWER AWAY

Once you know what others are going to do, you can take away the power they control over you. Instead of being shocked, you take it as par for the course.

What I have found is this: It's very important to be mindful of who you share your big ideas with. When you share with your family members, friends, and loved ones, you are trusting they understand your idea and are good at business and assessing risk versus reward. Let's face it, most family members do not have the skill set to analyze what you are trying to do properly. So, naturally, they are not going to go along with your crazy and wild ideas.

Most family members are not equipped to handle entrepreneurial ideas. Typically, they have normal jobs and work for someone who is the boss. What happens is fear grips them and yields them powerless to make informed decisions.

The costliest advice you will ever receive is free advice. It is generally useless, and like mentioned above, based upon fear and not knowing what you are talking about.

When you have a big dream or big goal, share it with someone who is more entrepreneurial in spirit. Better yet, someone successful in the same type of business. When you share ideas, they can help guide you, share ideas with you, and help you with bigger and more grand ideas. Mentors can help you go down paths of crazy possibilities and get input together on how to accomplish these goals. There's so much you can do when expressing to people who know the business, are in the business, and see the business in the same way you do. What starts out as a dream can turn into something absolutely attainable on another level. I find you will have a much better response and it will help guide you in that decision making process. This is because what you're really wanting from them is advice such as:

- Will this work?
- Does my business strategy make sense?
- Do I have the resources for success?
- Have I considered all the risks?
- Can you guide me?

Most successful entrepreneurs will encourage you in your journey. Yes, sometimes you have to fail and screw things up to succeed. You see, for most of us, we learned from our success stories, but more importantly, we learned from our failures. Knowledge, true knowledge, is the summation of all your successes and failures together. In a simple word: Experience.

Again, remember that people will always let you down no matter where you're at in your life. They will put you down, they will tell you no, they will be brutally honest as to what their opinion is. This is normal. In the sixth grade, I did not know this, and it almost beat me down. Thankfully for me, my father was my cheerleader. He told me I could always do whatever I put my mind to and that I was special. His desire was for me to be better off than he was. I had my doubts, but I kept moving on.

Big Idea:

People will always doubt your ability—don't listen to them.

In my life, there have been many people who told me I could not succeed in this or that. I've learned never to take it personally. Most of these people want you to succeed and will come around. When you do make it, these same people will then tell you they always knew you could do it.

Let's travel into high school. I played middle linebacker in football, and during the season, I had practice five days a week from August to late November. I also had a part-time job mopping the floors from 7:00 pm to 11:00 pm four days a week at the local grocery market called Ramey's.

Who has time for homework? I barely had time to socialize and relax. I know a lot of people who can look back on their high school experience and tell similar stories. By the time it came to studying, my brain was toasted marshmallows squished between chocolate and graham crackers—and it showed. My math grades were slipping to the point where repercussions were coming. I had to make a change and fast.

That change came in the form of making Kevin Highfill, the smartest kid in math I knew, a deal he couldn't refuse. So, every morning after sleeping in first hour, I would rush into second hour and start copying my homework . Thanks to Kevin, I graduated.

Now, I know my teachers are reading this book, and they probably know I copied because all my answers were the same as all the smart kids I sat behind. But I do want to **stress** I only copied from the smart kids. Now, I did not cheat on a test, but I copied homework like a pro. This became one of life's biggest lessons for me and the reason I'm writing this book.

It's called "Copy Your Way to Success" for a reason. For me, I started copying in high school. When I needed that math homework done, and I did not have it completed, I would find a classmate in the classes before math class and try to get their homework so I could copy it. Now, fortunately for me, believe it or not, I have a very strong mind, and I'm fairly good at remembering facts, figures, and data.

So, while I was in class, I would listen to all the instruction and do as much homework as I possibly could. However, once that bell rang, I was done with that hour of class. There was no doing any more homework.

I left high school with a lot of B's. I never really applied myself, but I did stumble upon my greatest gift, and that is the ability to copy successful people.

Big Idea:

Don't be a maverick. Learn from others.

I always got more from taking simple ideas I knew worked and implementing them in my business. It will work for you too.

This lesson keeps repeating itself in my life, and truly, I believe it's a gift. I learned later on from Tony Robbins what I was doing in my business was called "Modeling Success."

By modeling others' success, I have been able to do amazing things. Because I felt I wasn't that smart, I have always surrounded myself with people who were much better than me, and I've learned to do the things they did that were successful and to not do the things they didn't do. This is another big idea.

Big Idea:

Do what successful people do . . . and don't do what successful people don't do.

I can't stress this enough. People are always looking for that quick fix or done-for-you product, but most of the time, it's just daily habits, consistency, and getting work done. Most successful people have systems that work for them. Find those systems and implement them in your life. Things will change.

LEARNING THE GAME OF LIFE

ONCE I WAS OUT of high school, I had my heart set on going to UNLV in Las Vegas. Upon arriving there, I knew I needed a job. It just so happened I was a certified lifeguard. The second hotel I talked to gave me a job. To this day, I consider it the best job ever.

Say hello to the Stardust Hotel & Casino Pool Boy.

This next story is called the HUSTLE.

Back then, this job was cool. It's not like it is today at pools in Vegas. We ran our pool like perfect clockwork with our focus always on the money. We never had chaise lounges sitting by the pool empty.

We kept all our lounge chairs close to our sign in desk.

This was done for a reason.

Whenever someone left the pool, that chair was picked up quickly and put back in our stack. We did this for one reason and one reason only: money.

You see, to get a lounge chair at our pool you needed to check in. That meant giving us your name and room number. The truth is, we never cared if you were a hotel guest. We wanted you to see the big, clear plastic jar with money in it that said "tips."

Upon signing in, we would then ask how many in your party. Most people would say two. So, then we would go over and put four towels around one arm and then grab two lounge chairs and swing them over our back and proceed to ask the hotel guests, "Where would you like to sit?"

You see, at the Stardust Pool, we gave you service.

Once you pointed your best spot out, we walked you over there and put your lounge chairs out. Next, we tried to make some small talk as we unfolded a fresh white towel on the bottom of the lounge chair and hooked another towel through the top bank of the lounge chairs, then smoothly pressed it down to make it look neat and professional.

At this point in the process, people generally get the idea. They have fumbled either with some chips in their pocket or given us a couple dollar bills. We called it getting "greased," and we loved it.

Every morning, the pool opened at 8:30 am, and we always had a line. Before we even started, we pulled out that tip jar, opened it up, put a dollar in it, and made sure we slammed the lid down so everyone looked at it. Then we opened the pool for business. We would take our time with each person in line being kind and courteous while finding their spot at the pool. Once "greased," we would haul butt back to the sign in desk for the next person, then the next. This was a well-oiled machine, and I think people loved watching us do it.

Occasionally, you'd get the oddball who wanted to screw with us and thought he'd cut in line and get a lounge chair himself. This was never a good idea. Once we saw even an inkling of a guest thinking they were going to grab a chair, all my fellow lifeguards' sixth sense kicked in, and everyone immediately stopped, turned, and stared. The lifeguard who was closest to the chairs had the duty and privilege to stop this kind of atrocity without remorse. Using his authoritative voice, he would say something like, "Sir, sir, you are not allowed to handle these lounges. Please get back in line, and we'll seat you as soon as possible."

Most of the time, this worked. But, it was Vegas, and everyone has a moment when they want to rage against the machine. This is where the guest insists he's going to do it his way. That's when everyone drops what they are doing and starts walking toward our chairs, and if you are closest, you go grab that chair out of the guest's hands. Once you had ahold of the chair, we would automatically turn into wonderful pool boys and ask the guest where he would like to be seated and go about our business.

Occasionally, we would have a "whale" come to our pool. A "whale" was anyone willing to give us a five-dollar tip. To us, it meant you just became royalty, and you would be getting our VIP treatment. Upon getting your towels done on your chaise lounge, and you showed us a "fin" as we liked to call it, we would immediately run back into our poolroom and produce, wait for it . . . the COCKTAIL table. No other guest had any idea we had these tables. We kept them hidden from sight so other guests could not snatch them. The only way, and I mean the only way, you could get this table was with a fin. No exceptions. Now, for the guest getting this table, their status just went up tenfold. No one else had a cocktail table, and no signs were stating we even had them.

Not only did it get you a cocktail table, you now had special privilege use of our special and exotic lifeguard lotion. We had specially formulated our own lotion taken from different name brand products. We took the best moisturizing lotions we sold, and we mixed it with the best tanning oil. The result was our special formula that people loved. We would always offer our lotion whenever the fin was presented.

Always . . .

Not everyone got our system. We would have one or two guests a day request a cocktail table. Of course, these tended to be the people who stiffed us as well. We would tell them that we were out. We couldn't say they cost five dollars because the hotel would never allow that, but we would simply say we didn't have any more. Or better yet, when you reached the point of enlightenment as a pool boy, you would respond with your Ancient Secret Wudan Shaolin Monk response and say "You have to be smart about it." If the grease came on second or third try, that would allow you a shoe-in and get you a table. But, you would need to be smart the next day as well, or no table for you.

Day in and day out, we would work our pool and collect tips. At the end of the day, we would total the amount collected from the two pools at our hotel and distribute the money. On average, we would end up with approximately $80 to $100 dollars each day we worked. Now I have to remind you that I was eighteen years old and for me, this was a lot of money. The best part about this job was that we never had to report our tips. This money was sweet. Plus, we were making $4.25 minimum wage as well. That meant in total, I was making $18.00 dollars an hour, if you take I was paying no taxes on my tips, and I had few bills. The only things I had to pay was my rent at $350 a month and my truck payment $325 a month, gas and utilities. The rest was for me to blow, and guess what, I did. Every month I seemed to go through $2,000 dollars of disposable income.

Looking back, I want to quickly point out that all the systems we put in place at the pool I never created. I was taught them, and I put them into practice.

We had a system for how we ran our pool and principles we held dear. All I had to do was buy into the idea that these systems would work, and then I carried them out throughout the day. What it did for me and my fellow lifeguards is, it put cash into our pockets. Every other pool my friends worked at made less than $30 bucks a day in tips, and their hotels were much bigger and nicer. What I learned is people will always pay for quality service, and it usually is *systems* that bring this service about.

BIG IDEA:

Most skills are teachable.

Always be on the lookout for systems that yield big results. It's in those systems that true wealth can be discovered.

Now, I'm not very proud of the way I handled money in my pool boy years, but for the record, it was the best three summers of my young life. I did a lot of neat things, and I blew a lot of money on stupid stuff, and like all Vegas stories, I left broke.

Although leaving broke, I learned some of life's most valuable lesson in those three years. These lessons are the kind not taught in school, and I believe what has given me the edge today.

It's called street smarts.

Big Idea:

You don't need a college degree to have smarts. Many times in life, common sense goes a long way.

Most people think a college degree is THE ONLY way to success. I believe that used to be true. There was a time when a college degree meant a lot, for not many people attended a college. Now, it seems, everyone has one and many are not successful or even working in the field they studied. Not to mention all the debt that comes with that piece of paper. What's more important nowadays, in my opinion, is experience.

As a young man on his own, I learned to hustle early. I hustled tips at the pool by giving great service. My job was to make the guest feel special and appreciated. When a guest asked for something out of the ordinary that wasn't the typical ask, I would go out of my way to make it happen.

For example, there was a guest who wanted lunch from a special restaurant in the hotel. Now the pool offered certain items to eat, but this item was not on the menu. Now, to remind you, I'm just the pool boy. I'm not a cocktail server that serves food and beverage. This guest asked my cocktail waitress for the item, and she says it's not available on our menu. At this point, I'm thinking to myself, what a huge mistake.

She leaves and leaves the guest upset, and I can tell they are not happy. It's VEGAS baby, and if you want something, damn it, somebody should make it happen. Well, guess what happens next? Yours truly comes to everyone's rescue.

I'm a problem solver. I realize that the cocktail waitress doesn't know this guy is a "WHALE," i.e., big tipper, and he has asked for something special.

I go up to the guest to find out exactly what he wants and take the order. Next, I go to the cocktail waitress and make a deal with her. She's unwilling to get this guy's lunch at another place because it will take too much of her time to make it happen. She doesn't see the profit to be made by going above and beyond.

I take initiative and go to the restaurant that he wants food from in the hotel, and I find a server I know. I tell him I need a favor and give him a couple of dollars tip. I want him to order this food, and then once it's cooked, I asked him to please bring it to the pool.

Twenty minutes later, the guest's food arrives, but of course, it comes to me. I then hand deliver it to the guest and ask for his room number or credit card. He gives me his room number. I then make sure the server from the restaurant has this. I tell him I'll be over in ten minutes to collect the ticket the guest needs to sign.

I ran back over to the restaurant, picked up his ticket and delivered it to the guest who signed it. By the way, I had already filled the tip part out as CASH. Next, I hustled back to the server and gave him his ticket so he could close it out. What this did for the guest at the pool was, it made him happy. I was able to fulfill his request when everyone else said they couldn't. Maybe I had to break a couple of rules to do so in the process, but the hotel's golden rule was to make the guest happy. When the guest was about ready to leave for the afternoon, he called me over and began to tell me how much he appreciated what I did. Furthermore, it was his wife who wanted the item from the restaurant, and it made him look good. He then proceeded to give me a $10 tip, and his bill was only $20 at the restaurant.

Big Idea:

I define street smarts as being able to figure things out even when there are obstacles in the way.

Once you say it can never happen, you are right. It is only when you engage your mind and ask, how can I make it happen, that your brain works, and the process begins.

I learned a lot in Vegas. I learned if you wanted a good seat at a comedy show, you tipped the maître d' hard. I learned if you didn't want to wait in lines, you acted as if lines didn't matter to you. Do celebrities wait in line for stuff? No, they don't. If there was a line to catch a taxi, I would go straight to the taxi guy hailing taxis like I knew what I was doing. I would then proceed to tell him I was in a hurry and needed a cab right away, as I had a "fin" in plain sight so he knew what was in it for him.

I didn't make a scene. I just acted like I knew what I was doing and that I was special. Greasing the cab guy got me what I wanted, which was a cab right away. This lesson played out well for me later in life.

When I was dating my wife before we got married, we were living in Norman, Oklahoma, and a new club, Studio 54, was opening in downtown OKC. This club was a new type of nightclub where you had to be 25 or older to get into. It had only been open for a month, and I wanted to take her there and check it out. It was about a 45-minute drive from Norman, and we were both excited to check it out. But, what came next, I didn't expect . . .

Now I'm not sure about your significant other, but mine hates long lines. She hates waiting to get seated, she hates traffic, and she hates inefficiencies. When we pulled up to the club, I noticed what appeared to be the longest line I have ever seen wrapped all around three-quarters of the club's building.

Shelley started giving me sell signals right away, meaning she wanted no part of this. She started getting irritated as she told me to look at the lines, and how she just knew we would have to wait for hours to get in. She piled it on thick, but tonight I wasn't buying it. I knew she wanted in, and I did. too. The buzz was crazy about this place, and we wanted to check it out.

It was time for some of my STREET SMART Vegas skills to come into play. I was confident in what I was doing. You see, we had dressed up and were looking good. My wife had on a cute blue cocktail dress, and I had slacks and a blazer, black-on-black. We looked the part, now it was time for the performance.

Now, Shelley had no idea what I had planned, and I could tell she needed a lifeline or else this whole thing was not going to turn out right. She then looked at me with those puppy dog eyes and said, "Are you *sure* you want to go to this club and wait in line?"

I looked straight into her eyes, and with all my

confidence I responded, "Honey, we are not going to be waiting tonight."

A look of confusion went up and down her face as she tried to process what I had just said. She replied, "What do you mean not wait in line? The line is halfway around the building."

I took this opportunity to build a big "love deposit" in my then girlfriend's "love bank." After all, I was playing for keeps because I loved this woman and knew she was a keeper. I told her that she was special and she deserved to get into this club, and I was going to make it happen.

I could tell she wanted to believe in me, but everything she had seen seemed to contradict what I was saying. I mean, if there's a long line, and it doesn't appear to be moving at all, how in the heck could I command it to go faster? I didn't know anyone in the line, and it was doubtful anyone would let us cut in.

I grabbed Shelley's hands, pulled her closer to me, then gazed deep into those dark brown eyes, and I asked her a simple question. "Do you believe in me?"

It took her a second to compose an answer, then she gazed back into mine and said, "Yes, I do." I then told her to follow me and follow my lead and to not look at anyone in the line. Just follow my lead and own it.

We started walking toward the front of the club hand in hand. Not too slow, not too fast, more like we were walking confidently toward the front of the club. Shelley walked straight ahead and was following my instruction being oblivious to anyone in line. We walked together, but she let me be slightly ahead letting me lead. I could feel the eyes upon us like daggers piercing through our backs, gazing as to who were we to be walking past everyone and not even paying attention and not caring. I could feel the envy as they wished they were doing the same thing.

We walked past half the line because of the way our vehicle was parked in the parking lot. Each bold step we took brought us closer and closer to the entry. Each step drew us closer and closer to the person who was going to let us in: the doorman.

We turned the last corner of the building into a small straight path and 20 feet straight ahead was the doorman. I immediately locked eyes with him and smiled, as we continued to walk with purpose toward him. I had Shelley close to my side as we held hands walking past everyone until we finally stopped right in front of him. I then nonchalantly pulled my ID from my pocket and held it out to the doorman and calmly stated that I was on the VIP guest list. He grabbed my ID, looked at it for a moment, then checked the list that had a bunch of names written on it. He scanned for just a minute and then said confidently, "Mr. Johnson?" I replied, "Yes." He then said, "Right this way." We proceeded to walk past what seemed like a mile of people standing in line waiting for a chance to get into this hot new club. Shelley and I did not wait at all. We were being treated like royalty.

So what had just happened in that brief minute or two exchange with the doorman? Why did he just let me in, and why did he think my name was Mr. Johnson?

What I learned from being street smart is how people make their money. I studied people, and I was always curious. Because I used to work at a hotel and casino that had a club, I had made it a point to shop talk with the bouncer. I had let him know I worked at the hotel, too, as lifeguard. I would talk about my tips and how things worked. Then I would ask him, does he ever get to make tips, or do people try and buy their way in? He looked at me with a big smile on his face and told me, "Why do you think I have this job?" He worked at a gym during the day, and this was how he made extra weekend money. It was all about the gratuity.

Me being curious, I started asking how much to get in. What were the rules to the game? Remember, I knew it took a "fin" to get the VIP at my pool. What did it take to get into the club? What I learned is that it's all about confidence and not causing a scene. If you are with a beautiful girl, and it's just you and her, it's not as pricey. If you have a small group, it's going to cost a little more. Furthermore, if you have a big group of "guys only," it will never work.

What I'm talking about is the grease.

Big Idea:
Be curious in all matters of your life.

You can learn more than you could ever imagine learning from others.

What Shelley did not see was, as we exited our vehicle, I had grabbed my wallet and pulled out my driver's license. I then proceeded to fold two $20 bills behind it neatly. At that point, I put both money and license in my left pocket and started the walk with Shelley. The reason I told Shelley not to look at anyone in the line, to only look forward was because that's what celebrities do. You see, we had to act as if we were celebrities and play the part. I mean, why else would all those people let us get in front of them and not cause a scene? We didn't seem in a hurry. We acted as if we were owners of this place and we were coming to get in.

Remember, I smiled at the bouncer. This was done intentionally. I needed him to smile back and get through his tough demeanor. Once in front of him, I pulled out my driver's license and held it with both hands, presenting him my card. I kept the card low so as no one would see what was underneath. Cold hard cash. I knew when the bouncer grabbed my card, he knew what was going on as he felt the greenback. He looked back at his list then magically took one hand and swept below the card as the other hand passed the license back to me. I knew Shelley and I had played the part and looked it, too. People were looking at us, and the bouncer knew that too. He took his time looking again, over the list, as to appear he was scanning for my name. You see, he was playing his part also.

That, my friends, is how I made my wife a believer. As we got into the elevator to go to the top floor, only she and I were in it; she looked at me and said she couldn't believe what had just happened.

Here we were, just her and me, riding to the top floor. I'm not going to lie, pulling that off felt amazing. Seeing the look in Shelley's eyes after was all I could ever hope for. I want everyone to know I'm not making this up. This did happen, and I was confident that it would, but I was also terrified that it wouldn't work out. But I had to try. I had to put it out there and see if I could do it. I had done it before in Vegas, and I had a good feeling it would work in Oklahoma City, too.

Big Idea:
Act as if you already have it.

The most important things in life happen because you believe in them. Make it a point to visualize your dreams and goals and know they are within your grasp.

I truly believe the reason I was able to pull that off was because I was confident. You have amazing power, but you have to believe in yourself. Nothing in life is given to you, yet you can put things in motion in your life, and the first part of the motion is your belief.

The reason I'm writing this book now is I finally believe in myself enough to write it. I know it will be a best seller. I tell myself daily how many people I can touch, how many people will hear my story and be changed, how many people will start on a new path that will lead them to success and fulfillment.

What you believe is so powerful. You have to act as if you already possess what you want. You have to be working toward the goal daily. People do change. I see it all the time.

Let's take smoking for example. Most people understand the dangers of smoking, and many want to stop. They know if they quit, it will probably prolong their life and for sure save them money. Now let's look into the psychology. If you were to say, I'm going to try and quit smoking. How powerful is that? It's weak . . . The great Yoda in Star Wars said it best. "Do or do not, there is no try." When you say "try," it comes from a belief that it's not possible, that it's very hard, or "I hope I can do it." The problem with these statements is you're already giving yourself an excuse.

Now, think about making this statement. I quit smoking. Isn't that a shift in mindset to make that statement? Let's talk about how you feel if you said, "I quit smoking." That's the way of the warrior. That's an "I am" statement that tells others your intension without need for interpretation. People quit smoking, but lots and lots of smokers try . . . to quit. The ones who actually quit are the ones who make up their minds, make the bold statement in their minds and then never look back.

At the height of my second year of being a pool boy, I wrote down a poem I've always held dear to me. I wrote it when I was nineteen, and I have it committed to memory today.

It's about the struggle and urges to succeed and all the dark paths of the unknown. It's about finding one's true self. I hope you enjoy this.

Blinded by the deepest dark
And lost in all my ways
Where will I go tonight
Better yet, where will I stay

I know I can
And for sure I must
Fulfill my dream
It's all or bust

The light
It seems so dim and extremely small
I want to get there
But afraid I'll fall
Keep trying, they say
You know you can
I must succeed
And fulfill my plan

Though at times I feel like crying
Let down by all the rain
I control my destiny
I control the pain

They say if you want it bad enough
Your dreams will see you through
Just wish upon a shining star
And they will all come true
So now I've found my way in life
The dark has all but left
And those times that were tough and hard

Those memories are the best

Now you may have fame and fortune too
You may have it all
But watch out for that little guy
'Cause he may make you fall

You see, you got here the easy way
Daddy put you on your feet
He gave you clothes and everything
Which my dad can't compete

So I've clawed and scraped my way
To all that I've become
And if you think you can deal with me
You're just another bum

They say that wealth is a rich man's obsession
And a poor man's dream
But love is what it's all about
It's rare and hardly seen

'Cause you may make all the wealth
That may seem so true
But does that make you happy
Is that really you?

If wealth is what this world's about
Then we must all be blind
'Cause it is like my mother said
Good men are hard to find....

I wrote that poem in the summer of 1994, and it still means something to me today. At that age, I wasn't sure what I was supposed to do or what my life's mission was. I just knew I wanted to be successful.

And I knew it was going to be up to me to get it done. At the tender age of 19, I already knew there would be pain and struggle to succeed. I'd have to hear a lot of no's.

Now that you know a little backstory, let's speed things up to the good stuff. This next part is when I got the **download from the mothership** and realized what I was meant to do.

BRUCE WAYNE

WITH NO DEGREE OR formal education, I believe you have about three options: get a trade, manage some stuff, or sell some stuff.

I sold used cars for around four years until Shelley called one day and said she couldn't marry a car salesman. She wasn't kidding either. By the end of that day, I had scheduled an interview for a restaurant manager. Of course, I got the job because I was a good car salesman and sold my skills and ability.

I thought I worked a lot of hours in the car business, but it doesn't even come close to the restaurant game. I was making my fiancée happy by having security, but at what price? I continued bearing this burden, but every day, I felt more and more trapped in a job that had no end I would be proud of.

So now I had reached a certain point in my work life. I think a lot of people get to this place I am going to describe and talk about. It's a place where you are just plain frustrated.

You're frustrated with the people you work with, and you're frustrated with yourself. I hated my job. I was making okay money, but not great money. When I looked at my boss, he seemed miserable and stuck. When you get to this place, I think a lot of people tend to self-destruct.

That's kind of what I did. I got to a place where I started eating a lot and not working out. I became overweight. I wasn't happy with my appearance or my image. I just wasn't happy with my life. It wasn't turning out the way I had planned.

I looked at rich people, and I knew a lot of wealthy people, they lived an entirely different lifestyle. I wished, I mean I wished I had that lifestyle. I remember my wife and I would drive in neighborhoods and be looking at these nice, beautiful, custom homes and saying, "Man! What do these people do? How do they afford it? How can they afford a home like this? They're rich!" Then, we'd go back to our small little home.

At this point, I didn't have much money. I didn't feel like I had any time freedom. I always had to clock in. And you know, time is important.

I was disgusted with myself, as I asked myself, "Is this it? Is this as good as my life gets?"

Then, I started questioning myself, "Do I just need to go back to school and get a degree so I can get a better paying job?" I was living paycheck-to-paycheck, I think like most people in their early 30's. I didn't like it. I mean, I wanted more. I wanted a lot more; in fact, I WISHED for more. We wished, my wife and I, we used to wish we could own a really big custom home.

Your beliefs become a reality, and when you have a wish, it means you don't think it's possible.

Big Idea:
Wishing for things in life is fruitless.

If you want something in your life, stop wishing and start believing. So many people wish things will happen while never understanding how some people make things happen.

So, there was a lot of pain, a lot of self-doubts, pity, and I felt sorry for myself. I had started looking back on my choices and was frustrated with myself and the choices I had made. I was not the young boy in the poem I had written when I was 19. Life had taken ahold of me, and things were not going as planned.

You see, at this point in my life, I felt how a lot of people feel: trapped.

I think everybody goes through this at some point in their life. They have doubts and fear. That fear can cripple you. You want to be somebody, but you're so afraid you're not. When you look around, people are not encouraging you, they're telling you you're not somebody.

What's worse is you don't dream big anymore. That kid who used to dream wildly without boundaries is now locked in the basement of your mind. You don't dream and start talking to yourself as if you could achieve it. You start making excuses.

Not only was I miserable to myself, I think when we get into this mode, you're also miserable to others. My wife would tell you I was a big SOB a lot of times, and I was.

I was not winning husband-of-the-year awards in this period. I was in a daydream going through the motions like a zombie. Most people start out with a desire, but as life flexes its muscle, they start to hide it, and then eventually people forget desire was ever there. It's then that they accept defeat and live out their miserable lives.

Luckily for me, a spark happened that changed everything.

During my time of despair, frustration with myself, and everything I was doing, I knew I needed to change.

I got a gift from my mom. My mom remarried a man named Bruce. I now call him Bruce Wayne. He's not Batman, but he was loaded.

On our way to lunch with my mom and Bruce, aka Batman, my mom turned around and said, "Honey, how would you two like to come to Hawaii with us? You see, Bruce has a home in Hawaii, and they had just offered us a vacation of a lifetime.

Better yet, Bruce's house was located in Kauai, the Garden Isle, which is probably the most beautiful place on earth as far as I am concerned.

Let me share what I believe is heaven on earth.

This mystical place is the place that took a grown man and somehow breathed life back into his dreams and goals. This place allowed a flicker of light back into my life. It allowed that young boy who grew up on the farm and used to dream big dreams come back into my heart.

Hawaii is magical.

I remember stepping out of the airport and smelling that tropical air. It smelt so alive and wild. I took in huge breaths, drinking it in and feeling intoxicated with life and vigor. Then, my eyes looked out and saw the mountains get lost in the clouds above.

It felt so pure. Mystical and magical is the only way I can describe it. I've never seen anything so beautiful, so majestic, and so alive and vibrant. I was moved by this island that I wrote a poem to express how I felt watching my first sunset.

The Falling Sun

Sunset, O how beautiful you be
Innocent and refreshing
Filling my restless heart with longing desires
Romantic light
Soft and delicate as a red rose
Blessing the open sky so bold and beautiful
Cool breeze swiftly blowing me far, far away
What's out there, what lies beyond
Mystical and magical a feeling of freedom
No worries to taint this
Burning heart of mine
Let go of my will destined to fly high
To soar like an eagle
With grace and pride
Hovering high above this world watching all
below
I am a man
A man with fire in his eyes
And wind beneath his wings
Free of all restrictions let go of society
A creature of the wild
Answering to no man but me
I am in control
I fly upon my chosen path
Uncertain as to where I'll end
Tomorrow, a new day full of hope and ambi-
tion
A promise to do what is right
The pulsating rhythm of the powerful ocean
Waving goodbye to the glowing sun

The taste of the salty air
The smell of marine life
The echo of birds playing in the distance
Feeling the moist sand oozing between my toes
Goodbye Sunset
O how beautiful you be

I was ready for change because at this point in my life, I needed to feel worthy. I didn't want to continue on the same path. I wanted more, but for a brief period settled. Stepping foot in Hawaii changed me in ways I can never explain.

Shelley and I got into Bruce's car, as he and my mom picked us up at the airport. We drove 30 minutes northeast to a place called Anahola. We knew Bruce had a home in Kauai. However, we had no idea that it was located right on the beach. Mom and Bruce did us a solid by not telling us and letting us experience it.

As a young boy, this house is what I dreamt paradise would have looked and felt like. In fact, I never had visions or images of how this place felt. It was somebody's home, not a hotel. It was a private place of paradise, and I got to enjoy it with Shelley. Looking out from the back patio all you saw was beautiful ocean and the magic sound of waves crashing onto the shore. It sat maybe 50 feet from the ocean. You walked out the back door and then went over the sand berm. You had waves crashing in front of you as the wet sand oozed between your toes reminding you you were in paradise.

It gets better. Not only was this house on the beach, this house was on a cove.

As Shelley and I walked the beach early the next morning before the sun had woken up to kiss the powerful waves of the ocean, we found another surprise. About 300 feet up the cove from Bruce's house, we witnessed a fresh river from the tropical mountains that ran right into the ocean.

As we crossed the river, the sun decided to start its journey and bring light into the day. I was mesmerized as the spray from the waves breaking was somehow transformed by the sun. I will never forget that morning. That morning, God had put his finger on my heart and said "Be still..."

I stood there hand-in-hand with Shelley as we took in the sunrise, being both captivated and transformed at the same time. It was as if the scales of the old life we were living had finally run its course, and we were shedding that skin and life.

A new day indeed had begun, and the scales over my eyes had been removed. I spent over an hour in that spot with Shelley as joy filled my heart. In that time, I focused and realized all the things I was grateful for. It wasn't that life was bad. It had been the way I approached it with my mind. I vowed that day never to let stinkin' thinkin' corrupt my heart or dreams again.

Big Idea:

The power of your mind is EVERYTHING!

Don't be the victim of "stinkin' thinkin'." Even when all seems impossible, tell yourself that you can and you WILL. You will be surprised by the results.

That week, Shelley and I had the time of our lives. As our vacation approached the end, I walked that beach one more time. I stood still again and watched the sun come up. Then I looked over at Bruce's house. I thought to myself, who is Bruce? How does he have this home, and what does he do?

I had never seen wealth like this before. How did he make it? Was he born with it in his family? Could he give me clues on how I could achieve the same wealth?

'Cause I saw a man, who had TIME & MONEY. Most people have one or the other. People with a lot of time seem to not have much money, and people with a lot of money tend to not have much time.

Bruce's house had fine art in it. He had nice cars. He also had three more properties on the island. More importantly, Bruce's phone was not ringing. He didn't appear to have any cares or worries. Bruce had it both, time and money, and you could see the difference in the way he carried himself. I remember thinking to myself, this was how I wanted to feel some day. I wanted to have enough money coming in to not worry about the thing most people seemed consumed over.

I had to figure out what Bruce was about.

I mustered up all my courage and finally went

up and asked him what he did and how he made his money.

He replied that he was in real estate and he owned apartments.

Me, not understanding what that meant, asked a clarifying question. "So you're a realtor?" I asked. Bruce looked at me as if irritated and replied, "No, they work for me."

Bruce may not have been a perfect human, and he didn't unlock the mystery of real estate for me, but I left the island thinking he was the Big Kahuna...

He had given me a perfect vision of what time and money should look and feel like.

Six months later, I read this book called *Rich Dad Poor Dad* by Robert Kiyosaki, and all the light bulbs in my head were going off. I finally understood what Bruce did.

Bruce was a real estate investor, and he owned apartments that gave him cash flow.

Around five months after reading that book, and every book I could get my hands on, I boldly charted a new chapter in my life. In June of 2005, I created my company, starting with the end in mind. Kahuna Investments was born.

I was so excited to start this new journey. I had read so many books filled with ideas and ways to make money in real estate. The only hard part was figuring out the best strategy. It took a while, but I finally decided to follow a book that said to take out a home equity loan and use that money to buy properties. So that's exactly what I did. I was able to get a $25k line of credit using our house as equity.

Now I had to solve the problem of finding a deal.

One book I had read talked about calling on banks and asking for their REO Department. For me, this sounded like a good idea, except I was really scared about going into a big bank. I had another idea. When I was in the car business, representatives from credit unions would always call on the dealership trying to get them to use them for loans on cars. They seemed different from the big banks that called on the dealership. They were much friendlier and way more approachable.

I opened the telephone book, yes—this was a while ago—and I started calling credit unions and asking for the REO Department. It didn't take long. By the fourth call, I called American Airlines Federal Credit Union and was transferred to Holly Lane. Holly was awesome. American Airlines had a maintenance facility in the area which meant the Credit Union was doing business in Tulsa. Holly had a couple of properties she needed to get rid of.

And just like that, I had a deal.

BIG IDEA:

Sometimes you may not have all the answers, but start moving toward your goals. Things seem to happen when you take action.

When you're willing to go outside your comfort zone, even when you may not have all the answers, growth happens. If you wait to figure it all out, sometimes opportunities will pass you right by. Don't be afraid of failing. That's part of the experience, and you will need some of it.

On my first deals, I decided to do all the work myself. I want to tell you right now, that was a bad idea. After doing three deals with Holly with me doing all the work on the renovations I quickly learned I was about half good at everything. I sucked at drywall, painting and tile. I was becoming a jack of all trades and master of none. Worse, I was really tired. It took me three or four times to get things done correctly.

In six months, I had managed to buy and sell three homes successfully and make money. I realized I wasn't good with rehabbing properties, jack of all trades master of none, so I thought I'd buy properties for rentals. That way I wouldn't have to do so many repairs and could limit myself in the amount of work I was doing.

I kept calling Holly, and by the next three months, I had found three more properties. This time, I was focusing on cash flow. I made all three rentals, and I was able to do the work quickly and in short order. More importantly, I was able to put renters in them quickly.

Man, it felt great.

I was now becoming an investor.

I had rental properties.

I was so excited. I had taken what I had learned

in books and made it work. I felt like I was on top of the world. Kahuna Investments was doing big things . . .

Now in my delightment, I forgot to look at my bank account. I was getting thrown another curve-ball, and I didn't even know it. I bought three prop-erties, and I took my profits from my first three deals to pay for repairs and the 25 percent down the bank required.

My new problem was all my money was in these three rentals. What was worse is that I was only net-ting $350 per month per property. Now $350 is not terrible, but it's not great. The real problem was my ego. I wanted to be a full-time investor. So now I was making $1,050 a month, and that was if we had no repairs or vacancies.

This is the point that I think most investors who want to get into real estate quickly fall into. They use their own money, and once they are out of mon-ey, they have no idea how to go any further. Their only option is to wait to save up more money and then get another deal. I fell into the same category. I wasn't making enough money to do real estate full-time, and now I was forced to put my real estate dream on hold.

I felt defeated, I tried to keep my head up, but

inside I felt like I had failed. I didn't have a way to get any more capital, and we needed income from me to support my family.

BIG IDEA:

Life doesn't always go as planned.

Roadblocks will constantly be lurking around every corner. When they do, it will be a test of your growth and attitude. Stay positive and know this is why you are an entrepreneur. You find ways to win despite all the roadblocks.

I needed to find a new job, but this time I wanted to figure out a way to make money and learn more about real estate. This new job came in the form of a financial advisor with Edward Jones. I was able to land the job because I had shown the grit and will to do real estate. Edward Jones placed high value on being a self-starter, and I was able to demonstrate that concept with my real estate success.

I trained with Jones for four months and passed my series 7 and series 66 test. I was now a licensed financial advisor. What I loved about this job is that I had the best company in the industry teaching me all the ways of money. I learned about stocks, bonds, mutual funds, CDs, and all kinds of financial strategies. I learned about MONEY and how it works. Jones had a spot located for me in Phoenix, AZ, and I moved my family to the desert.

At that point, as I was learning about money, Jones was also teaching me something else. They taught me the power of networking. I found myself being in the right places where money hung out. I started to surround myself with smart people who had money . . . I learned how to network like crazy and to follow up with contacts. Edward Jones taught me how to be a businessman.

I wasn't a great salesman, but I was always able to grind it out. I started out as a "new new." This meant I was given no assets and no office. Edward Jones provided me with a game plan, a laptop, and a printer. My job was to go door-to-door and introduce myself to people in a target area and tell them about myself and my company. It took nearly two years of doing this door-to-door in a suit and tie until I had enough assets under management that Jones now felt I was not a risk. That's when they opened up the golden doors and provided me with my own office, furniture, and an administrative assistant.

We have now come to the point where I talked at the start of this book. We all remember 2008. The market crashed. Probably the biggest drop we will see in our lifetimes. Real estate in Phoenix crashed something crazy. It was scary, and it was real. I had clients close to retirement age, and all the planning they had been doing for retirement was now in shambles. I had clients sit down in front of me in tears. Their life savings were now worth half or less. Worse was, in order to move money into a safer investment, I had to charge them a fee, per Edward Jones.

My heart left the business I was in. Every investment I had made with anyone I knew was now in the toilet. It was a very hard time to be a financial advisor, as I had no control of the market. It was vicious.

I got fired from Edward Jones and decided to go all in with real estate. I didn't have all the answers, but I knew I was willing to do anything and everything. It was not an option to lose. I was determined to succeed.

I went home later that day excited and nervous at the same time. I had just committed to myself, but now I had to let my wife know my plan. Although I was going to do it no matter what, I needed my wife to allow me. She had to be on board with the idea. So I sat her down, and I exposed my desire and commitment to her. We both agreed it would not be easy, and we may have to make short-term sacrifices, but at the end of the day, Shelley looked me straight in the eyes and told me she believed in me. Then she said, "DO NOT FAIL." She knew what was at stake, yet she allowed me to go at it.

I will never forget that night. I was so scared and nervous. I wanted Shelley to believe in me, but I didn't know how she was going to take it. That night she gave me everything I ever needed. She believed in me. I could see it in her eyes, she really truly believed.

As I'm writing this, my heart is filling with emotion. It's hard to go back to that moment and not break down. I think about the countless hours and 3:00 a.m. nights analyzing properties trying to figure out how to get deals. It was all so new to me, and the pressure to perform and make a paycheck for our family was real. Through it all, Shelley never complained. I think about how I started this dream, put it on hold, had to find a job, then ultimately get back into real estate. Again, Shelley always had my back, and her belief was like a cloak of armor. This small town farm boy, the boy who used to believe he could be or do anything, finally had the right champion. My wife is the reason I'm successful. She has always showered me with her words of praise.

We would go on walks at the end of the day around the neighborhood, and she would listen to my trials and tribulations. Shelley's advice was always sage, and she never jumped on me when I made mistakes. She would just say, "I know you'll fix it." Also, the way she talks to her friends about me, the way she looks into my eyes, and the way she lets me know I'm her man is simply amazing. If you looked from my wife's eyes, you would never see my flaws.

Her belief in me has always been more than I could ever believe in myself. She pushed me to be the best me in every way. Even when I made stupid mistakes. Shelley would dust me off and mend my wounds and then build me up with her words of endearment. Without hesitation, she would then kick me back out the door and say, "Go get 'em…."

Not only did she support me emotionally, my wife brought home the bacon. She worked very hard as a pharmaceutical representative, and she was good. Shelley was always ranked number one or two in her company. Her income was the fallback. She played it safe in corporate, so I could be the risk in our relationship.

We have a book we call our "love journal." It's like a personal journal, but this is for our love letters to each other. When you feel moved to put in an entry, you write it, then deliver to your significant other so they discover it. Everyone likes a surprise. In this journal, I have many entries telling her, "One day I'm going to retire you."

Honey, if you're reading this book, just know you are my everything. You complete me in every way, and I cherish the ground you walk on. I would move mountains if only you asked. I thank you for believing in me when no one else would. You are my best friend, mother to my kids, and I get to call you my wife.

Big Idea:
A significant other can make a big difference.

As human beings, we all have emotions. Our minds are constantly telling us who we are, and at times, we are replaying the wrong tapes in our minds. The power of having someone you are emotionally close to being a cheerleader and encouraging you can be powerful beyond measure.

Once I had Shelley's approval, I went full speed ahead, and I have never looked back.

MY FIRST MENTOR

COMING HOME FROM STARBUCKS the day I made a choice to win in real estate, I'll never forget. That day, I committed never to look back and charge full-steam ahead. I was going to make this work or else . . . There was no doubt in my mind that I was going to do it. I just wondered how long it would take.

Now, I wish I could tell you I had huge success starting out and that I rocketed toward a successful venture, but that's not my story . . . I wasn't holding pocket aces . . .

The next day I woke up, I was scared shitless. All I had were questions and no solutions. I had questions like, what was I going to do? How was I going be successful in real estate? Better yet, my wife's question, when are you getting paid? This led me to grab a yellow legal pad. I needed to come up with a plan of action and take stock of what I had currently.

I started by listing what my strengths were:

- I was committed
- I was willing to do anything
- I had time to do it
- Fear was motivating me big time
- I was teachable and coachable
- I was ready to implement

Not a real star-studded strength list, but that's what I was working with.

Let me point out that the last bullet point is the one that got me going.

Commitment

I think when most people initially start out, they are committed, but I don't think we grasp what commitment means these days. People get married all the time and commit to each other, but once things go south, it seems this word, "commitment" goes out the door.

When I say I was committed, I was ready and willing to do anything. As long as it wasn't against the law, I was going to do it. That didn't mean only if things were good. It meant I was going to commit no matter what. I knew that if I quit, I would feel like a failure. I had the mindset that quitting was not an option. I had to succeed.

<u>Fear</u>

The next big one on the list for me was fear. They say only two things motivate you in life: pleasure or pain. Pleasure is a great motivator, but in my mind, pain is bigger. I knew I was committed to my wife and family. They were my life and the only thing that matter in this world to me. I knew I had to perform and take care of them financially. Now, don't get me wrong. My wife, she worked, too. It's not like we were helpless without me, but we needed income from me to survive.

They were counting on me, and the fear/pain of losing them or letting them down was a great motivator to get me off my rear end and into action.

Teachable and Coachable

I'm not sure why, but I find most people are not teachable and coachable. I've never understood this. The fact that you are reading this book automatically makes you special. You are seeking knowledge. Most people think they have all the answers and have a know-it-all mentality. This is stupid thinking. You should welcome knowledge openly. By that, I mean you do not simply just think what's wrong with it or how you can improve it. Sometimes it's better to concentrate on the information and taking it all in and be a good sponge. It's only after receiving all the info without judgment that you can then tailor it to how it fits for your business. Being teachable and coachable is a must in business. Especially in the Information Age, as things change all the time.

Ready to Implement

It's one thing to consume great information. It's another to implement the ideas and strategies. I have been to so many seminars, workshops and webinars where I see the same people showing up time and time again. Sometimes, it's years in between events. When I ask them how things are going, they are still stuck at Step Number 1.

Why?

The answer for most is they feel like they need more information. Crazy, right?

This one thing, being able to implement, is the difference between success and failure for most individuals. Successful people understand that version one is better than version none. You don't have to have everything perfect to be successful. Sometimes you need to get into motion and start doing things. You may not have it perfect, but by putting things into action, good things seem to happen.

The next thing I did was write down all my weak points.

- I didn't have much money
- I had bad credit
- I was only book read, uneducated in the business
- I had no mentor

Taking stock of where I was financially, I knew I had to figure out a way to work with people and make things work.

No Money

This is a problem for 90 percent of the people reading this book, maybe more. When you start from the bottom, you don't have money. This is normal, so don't feel weird. Don't let it stop you. But money is a hard one to crack or get our mind around. When you don't come from money, you have to realize our minds have been programed from an early age.

Our parents used to tell us we will never be rich, but we have each other. Or, they would also say money isn't everything. These things are correct. Money is not evil, and the pursuit of it surely isn't.

The other thing about money is most believe you HAVE to have it. It takes money to make money.

Keep reading because I'm going to destroy this myth.

It may take money, but it doesn't have to be your own money.

Trust me when I tell you this. If you become an expert in finding deals and investments that are profitable, the money will come to you.

If you have money or not, after your first one - two deals, you will soon be out of money. If you don't have money, you may have to work a little more to get there. For people who have money, congratulations, you will not have to work as hard doing sweat equity.

In the end, if you have money or not, after your first one or two deals, you're going to need to start getting smarter and more creative. This is where the real work will begin.

Not having much money is, in a way, a gift. It teaches you to be resourceful. Growing up, I always knew that I had to figure things out. I always felt that gave me a leg up on anyone I came against. I wear it like a badge of honor.

When taking stock where I was at financially, I had around 5k I could spend, and that was on a credit card. No money felt like it was going to be a problem, but I had read books about how you could get into deals with no money and no credit.

I just needed to know how to do that . . .

Bad Credit

I had filed for Bankruptcy in 2003. It takes ten years for that to go away from your record. You can imagine, I wasn't going to be going to the bank for loans. Lots of people lost their homes, and their credit was ruined during the Great Recession, too. This may be you. I know when I filed I felt miserable.

How did I get to this point, filing for bankruptcy? This seemed like another big obstacle in the way, but I knew I'd read some books on how you could buy homes with no credit. I just needed the details on how to get this done. I'm going to show you this is a nonissue as well. I thought at first this one thing would keep me ruined for years, but it's not the case, and I will show you how I overcame this.

Only Book Read

A big problem I felt like I had at the time was I had read all the books I could about real estate, but the problem was the info had seemed very outdated. They talked about strategies that had worked back in the day. What I needed was info from someone who had been there, done that, and is still doing it now. I needed info on what was working in today's market. So, I turned to Google and started asking questions. This leads me to my last bullet point.

No Mentor

When I started researching what was working

now, I listened to lots and lots of testimonials of successful students in real estate. The one common theme they all shared was they had a real-life mentor guiding them. They had a mentor. A mentor is the key to success. You can be book read as much as you like, but having someone who you can call and bounce ideas off of is priceless. You can get there without a mentor, but by having a mentor in your life, the process of becoming successful is ten times greater and faster. A good mentor can understand where you are going and has had the experience, aka making lots of mistakes to help guide you.

Fewer mistakes mean more progress and better decisions.

Big Idea:

Take stock of where you are at and what you have, then create the plan to succeed.

When you add up all your strengths and weaknesses and look at where you're at, planning a successful route is a lot easier, and it gives you a plan.

Now that I'd taken stock of where I was at, it was time to formulate a plan of action. I knew two things: I didn't know what I didn't know, and I needed a mentor. My biggest idol at the time was Robert Kiyosaki, and through a Facebook ad, his company offered a free workshop.

Guess who was going, me.

Of course, at that workshop, they pitched a three-day event for $500 bucks.

I said yes because the workshop was really good. It was giving me great info and ideas about some things that were working, but it didn't go into specifics. They promised more at the $500 dollar event.

The $500 dollar event was really good too.

At this event, they talked about different strategies and what may work for you. The next three days, they talked about each category a little deeper but still leaving lots out. By the end of the week, I knew what category I was going to do.

I fell into the wholesaler category.

Why?

It's because I had no money, no credit, and no track record. Meaning, if I found a deal, I couldn't buy it or finance it myself, and I didn't have people lining up to do deals with me. The only place that seemed reasonable to start was wholesaling. With wholesaling, you can lock up a deal in a contract, and then find people with money who will pay you a fee to buy that contract from you. You're sort of acting as the middle man. This is one of the least risky moves a real estate investor can make.

Looking back, rentals were probably the worst choice I could have made because my need was cash flow, and my rentals were not producing much cash flow each month.

I needed large cash flow coming in quickly that came with wholesaling.

That seemed like the right place for me, but . . . I still didn't know exactly how to start wholesaling . . .

For $3,000 dollars, Robert's Rich Dad Company would teach me how, or so they said.

Enter my first real big purchase of info products and education. Now, when I went into that system back then, the program was run by Russ Whitney. The program ended up being very badly managed.

Robert has since bought that company, and the training is really good. But for me, I was hoping to get a really good mentor or teacher that would show me the secret sauce, but what I got was a person who was probably a great teacher, but not a seasoned investor.

He had no real-life experience. You could tell he was a paid speaker and was teaching a concept he wasn't doing.

So, I had spent 3k on my education and came out with a big zero. I remember going to the two-day wholesaler course sizing up the speaker and was like, "This guy is going to teach me?" Like I said, this guy that was teaching and was just that, a teacher. He had barely done any deals and was all hype.

I'm about a month into this thing, and it's about this time where my wife is looking at me. She's not giving me the stink eye yet. She's still encouraging me to do it, but there's a little bit of doubt creeping in the armor, and I know I have to figure something out quick.

Big Idea:

When things are not working, make a course correction.

When you are not getting the results in life you are looking for, take a minute to rethink the plan. Sometimes you may need to make a slight adjustment. The path to success is not a straight line.

Although the course on wholesaling sucked, it wasn't without benefit. One thing they said to do was join REIA groups, "Real Estate Investor Associations." You guessed it; I joined my local REIA immediately. AZREIA, which I found out to be one of the largest REIAs in the country, would turn out to be a big win for me.

So now I'm networking with investors. I'm brand new in the business yet full of fire. I don't know what the hell I'm doing, but I'm going to meetings, meeting people, putting them in my database, finding out what kind of investments they do, etc. I didn't know it at the time, but I was building a buyers list of people who wanted deals.

But what I needed was to get paid . . .

As Bruce Lee would say, when the student is ready the teacher will appear.

Enter Bob Norton.

At this point in the timeline, I need to check in and tell you where I was at mentally before Bob Norton came into my life. The day I committed, I did not hesitate or waver in my convictions. Close to two months later, with no money being made, I still believed.

I believed whole-heartedly that I was going to win. I would wake up, look at myself in the mirror and tell myself positive affirmations. I would say things like, "You are a machine." "You will figure this out and be wildly successful." I just knew this to be true. Let me say this again. **I knew it to be TRUE.**

I was in motion. I was letting the world know I wanted success. I wanted to win, and I was willing to do whatever it took.

Failure was not an option, period, the end.

When the wholesaler guru who sucked said to put out bandit signs, I did it.

It didn't matter that I did it wrong. Like, I used big wooden stakes that I stapled cardboard stock paper onto. It didn't matter that I couldn't drive these damned stakes into the ground . . .

You may not know this, but in the desert, you better have a drill.

It didn't matter that when a big gust of wind came by, it would rip my flimsy sign stapled to the stake clean off. For me, I felt like I was in the game. I was doing things most people would never do. Yes, I failed horribly, but I got better and better. However, I never once, and I mean this, I never once DOUBTED MY SUCCESS.

Big Idea:
Do the work

Most people will get analysis paralysis, meaning they will read and never take action. Getting off your ass is very hard for most people. I find that successful people start working immediately when they have a goal. You may not always be right in your endeavor and may make mistakes, but your motions bring you closer to your goal.

I'm going to recommend a book called *The Answer* by John Assaraf & Murray Smith. He co-authored another the book called The Secret. Now for me, The Secret is a little too far out there. Its theory is "think, and it will come." I think that's a little bit of a stretch. As I've thought about winning the lottery for a long, long time, yet it's never happened to me. In John's book The Answer, this book is more like "think about it, do some work toward it, and it will come." The key **is working** toward your goal.

This is a big statement coming up, and I want you to take heart and listen to me.

- Everything I have needed, and I mean everything I have needed, has shown up the moment I fully committed myself to my goals and started working toward them.

So let's enter Bob Norton.

I found Bob Norton totally by accident . . . but was it? When I bought the Russ Whitney/Rich Dad program, I had access to their site that had links to threads where people would post their stories of success or where they needed help. Other investors would comment and let you know how to solve your problem.

One thread that I was following had posted lots of great content about wholesaling. His handle was

Royal T. One day, Royal T posted about this guy named Bob Norton that had a system called KISS Flipping. "Keep It Simple Stupid" Flipping. He gave a link to a free webinar that was going on the next day. Next day, I got on the webinar, and I knew immediately that Bob was different.

He was way different than the people who had been teaching me. He had been there, done that, and was doing it now. Bob was teaching me how to find deals using the MLS. It was simple, precise, and exactly what was working at the time.

Of course, I had to pay another $500 for his course, but I knew this was the one that was a game changer.

And it was.

Bob had a system that he knew worked and it worked in any city. Better yet, Bob had said he would do 50/50 split deals if you found a deal that met his criteria. That's all I needed.

<u>FOCUS</u>

I consumed all of Kiss Flipping in a four-day marathon.

All I did was eat, sleep, and breathe his course. Not only did I do that, but I also took action on all the action steps.

- Get MLS ACCESS
- Build List of REO Listing Agents
- Find Where Investors are Buyin
- Pick out five - six Neighborhoods and Know them inside and out
- Be lightning fast with your offer and make it easy

ACCESS

Step one was to get access to the MLS. I wasn't a realtor, but I knew one. I asked the realtor if she would be willing to allow me to have her access codes to log in. I told her I would do all the work researching deals, and I would allow her to write up all contracts. She saw what was in it for her and said yes.

Just like that, boom . . . I now had MLS access.

REO AGENTS

Next was building a list of REO agents. No problem there. Once I had MLS access, I just pulled that list. Bob taught me to cultivate the relationship with the REO Broker. What's funny is that Bob had

119

learned this skill from a good friend of mine now, Ron Walraven. Ron was an REO Broker back in the day, and he talked about how he liked working with investors that made his life easy.

Ron also talked about being quick offering the broker both sides of the listing and making sure you closed the deal.

HOT SPOTS

So now, I have access to a list of brokers, but I still need to find where Investors are buying. Again, very easy with the MLS. I used a feature in MLS to only look at Cash Sales for the last 90 days and mapped out my entire city. When that populated, I could easily identify pockets or cluster of sales in the city, and now I knew where the deals were at. Most cash sales are made with investors by the way . . .

KNOW THY NEIGHBORHOOD

I picked out a couple of neighborhoods that had lots of activity with cash buyers. Now, I needed to do my homework. Bob taught me how to pull comps and do massive amounts of research. I spent hours doing this. I got so good that when an REO broker had a deal in one of the neighborhoods that I tracked, I needed to know the square footage, if the property was in front or the back of the community, pool or no pool, one or two stories, granite or no granite. Once I had that info, I already knew how much I could offer on the property. I knew approximately my rehab cost and how much I could sell it for. I would make the offer on the phone with the REO broker, and he would write up the contract and get both sides of the listing.

This meant he made more money. That's what was in it for him, and I made it very easy for him.

BE FAST

By knowing my neighborhoods inside and out, it allowed me to be super-fast with offers and also proved to REO brokers that I was a professional. I took Bob Norton's information and put it into action. I now felt like I was becoming a real estate investor. I was in activity.

BUT I STILL NEEDED A CHECK!

With Bob's course, I copied exactly what he said to do. I never second-guessed it. I was completely focused.

Big Idea:

Do what other successful people do and don't do what they don't do. Don't try to screw up the process thinking you should do it your way.

I see so many new investors take information and want to change it immediately. They do these things, and they have no point of reasoning. I think it's a bad idea. Go through a course and do exactly as the mentor instructed. Once you've done that and experienced success, you can now make your tweaks.

I'm loving KISS Flipping, but I still needed to make money. Then one day Bob said to our group he would possibly partner with people and provide the capital if they had a smoking deal.

That was sweet music to my ears.

I pestered this man until I made him get in touch with me. In Phoenix, the market had crashed, and Bob would only do deals if they had the potential to make at least 30k profit. He offered to put all the money down and would split real profits 50/50. I saw where I was going to get paid. Bob had shown me the system on how to do it. All I had to do was implement the formula.

Guess what? I found all kinds of those deals and through it all, Bob Norton became my first real-life mentor. Bob taught me so much in a short period.

Bob and I did well. I listened to what he taught me and learned the business. More importantly, I was in the game. I was now doing real estate. I was no longer a spectator. I was calling REO brokers and short sale agents. I was researching subdivisions in the markets I did business with.

I was becoming an expert.

Big Idea:

Experts make money.
Generalists make excuses.

Work on becoming an expert in any industry you are working at and good things will follow. You will become a thought leader. Even though you have learned from others, most will hear it from you for the first time. Because it's through your filter.

Now, Bob taught a couple of invaluable things early on in my career. He said to document every deal you do with video and pictures. At first, I didn't understand why, but looking back now I'm certain. The power of images and video tell a story better than words can. Or in today's day and age, it's expected.

When you first start in this business, you will probably not have much of a track record. That was me. By using video you can show you know what you are doing.

Go to **https://youtu.be/KPJJ1ZXWo8c** and watch a video of a home I worked on with Bob Norton.

Even though Bob did this deal, used his funds and closed on it, it was my deal. I found it. I have proof, the video says so. This deal in Queen Creek, AZ was now my deal, and I could share this video with others to show them what I was up to.

I could say I was a wholesaler finding deals.

Bob and I did lots of deals that year, but I wanted to make all the money. The only problem was I didn't have any liquid funds. I had no funds. Things started taking off when I learned how to raise Private Money, or OPM (other people's money).

Up until this part, I was hustling and grinding

for survival. I had put this belief in myself, and that kid was still fighting.

It wasn't easy, and I had made so many rookie mistakes, but I had a spark. I knew that success was close, and I put my head down and stayed on task.

This brings me to my next big idea:

Big Idea:

You always pay the price. Success will never find someone who doesn't look for it and do the work.

You must master yourself before success shows up. It's in your daily routine and what you do. We don't become fat just by chance. To succeed, you must pay the price by saying no to the things that don't produce fruit to achieve your goals.

What I'm trying to say here is this: Life is full of choices, and when you make more good choices that help achieve your success, you will get there faster. Now, of course, we still need a work-life balance. But at times, my friends, it needs to be an all-out war . . . Sometimes you have to sprint and sprint hard. It's only then you can learn to marathon in between.

In the next chapter, please pay close attention. A lot of my limiting beliefs get shattered, and growth expands my entire being. That spark happened with Bob Norton. He started a fire that is burning to this day. The next chapter can define most everything I have done in my real estate career. It's real and important.

PRIVATE MONEY

THERE ARE TIMES IN your life when you look back and say right here, right here is when things turned around. For me, this couldn't be truer. I have experienced growth, but not like I'm about to share.

This one chapter can change your life. The title of this chapter says it all.

This is where a small-town boy learned a lesson that would shape the rest of his life and become the foundation that fuels his real estate growth. Life radically changed when I learned the power of Private Money.

I raised my first piece of private money totally

by accident and by doing so I uncovered something magical that has been my secret for raising millions of dollars from individuals.

It all started at my gym on a racquetball court.

I had been playing racquetball with a group of older men for three years or so, and every week, they would listen to my stories of real estate. One of the men I played with, Carl, was an ex-client I had at Edward Jones, and Carl liked talking about what I was doing.

He saw me start from scratch. He watched me get fired. He watched me go into real estate and struggle. He watched me get with Bob. Now I had his active attention on how things were going in real estate.

We always small talked in between matches, and I loved bouncing what I was doing off of Carl. He had good business sense and always offered me sound advice and his take on things.

One day before one of our matches, I was talking about the struggle I was facing to Carl. I was explaining to him I was getting really good at finding the deals, but I was still struggling with cash flow because of my agreement with Norton.

Now, I knew Carl lived in a retirement community, and because Carl was my client at Edward

Jones, I knew he didn't have large excess cash. Carl had planned his retirement perfectly. He had a pension and some assets that he put into annuities, and Carl was set. He was in retirement and had a lot of fixed assets that provided income, but he didn't have much liquid money. So I asked him this question, knowing I wasn't asking him for his money.

I was asking him for his help.

I looked at Carl and said, "Carl, you see what I've been doing, you know I know how to find deals. I want to make the larger part of the money, and I can pay the other part to an Investor as interest. Surely you know someone in the retirement community you live in that would like their money working a little harder for them." I then said, "Carl, would you mind helping me and asking around?"

Carl was cool and said he would try the best he could, but he had one question. He asked me how much interest rate I'd be willing to pay.

I told him I could afford to pay 12 percent rate of return and I could secure the money with a note and deed of trust. This was what Bob Norton was doing with the money he had been raising.

And just like that, we went on playing racquetball and had a great set of games. I didn't think much of it. I was hoping Carl would be able to find someone, but I did not count on it. Carl was my friend, and I didn't want to jeopardize what we had, so I didn't want to pressure him.

The next morning, guess who I got a call from?

You know it, Carl. When I answered the phone, Carl said, "Hey, Corey, you know that thing you were talking about yesterday, are you still wanting to do that?"

I responded, "Of course, Carl." In my mind I was thinking, I can't believe it, Carl found someone who wants to invest their money with me. Wow . . . Carl then said, "Corey, you may not know this, but I have a home that's completely paid for. I can borrow money from my bank at 3.2 percent, and if you give me 12 percent I can make a spread. How much money do you need?"

I just about fell over in my chair when I heard this. Did Carl want to give me his money? How could that be? I thought I knew where all his money was. I was totally beside myself. I quickly composed myself and gathered all my faculty, then calmly replied, "Carl, I need $85,000."

In which Carl quickly replied, "No problem, where do I send the money?"

My jaw dropped to the floor in total amazement. Someone that I knew just offered me $85,000. I was not prepared for that as I stuttered trying to figure out the next move. I hadn't been ready for that answer. It seemed like forever to get my lips to move, but finally, I replied, "Carl, let me get in touch with my title company, and I'll get you wire instructions."

Just like that, I raised $85,000.

I went on to do that deal and make a good amount of profit. More importantly, I learned something very, very valuable.

Big Idea:

You never ask people for money. You only ask people who do they know. The right people will self-select themselves.

This one big idea has opened up more capital than I could have ever imagined. Once you take the pressure off of asking people for money and are only interested in the people they know, it takes an enormous burden off the person you're talking to. By doing this, they now are critically paying attention, and the right ones always . . . always self-select.

Carl did something really big for me that day. He broke down a belief that I had carried as a child. Because I started out in a lower/middle-income family, it was hard for me to visualize people wanting to give me their money willingly. I had read numerous books on people that were able to get OPM, but I didn't think I would qualify. I didn't think I had the pedigree to take people's money. In that instant, I did it.

It was as if I went into a telephone booth as Clark Kent, and spun around and came out with my hands ripping my chest suit to reveal Superman.

When Carl wired that money to the title, I felt amazing like I was Superman . . . Yes folks, it's me . . . I may be deaf in my right ear, a little overweight, and talk out of one side of my mouth, but make no mistake, I'm a superhero.

Indeed, I felt like Superman. I had crushed a limiting belief that had been hounding me for so long of thinking I was not worthy. But I was worthy. I had put the time in. I was still willing to do whatever it took and was starting to have an extreme belief in myself. It had taken some time, but I was starting to see a pattern. For I started to see me as the person I had only dreamed about. I started to see myself as a businessman.

Carl, I know you are reading this book. Carl, you will never know how much that first investment changed me forever. I will always hold a special place in my heart for you. When no one else in the world was watching, you took a chance with me, and you have watched me grow and crush it.

If you want to see exactly how to get all the money in the world to fund all your deals, go to **www.KahunaWealthBuilders.com** and Opt-In for my free Quick Start Workshop Video Series. I have prepared a series of videos that show you how to unlock OPM in a way you never could imagine.

I quickly figured out you don't ask people for money, you only ask who they know. But, then I got curious. I knew I was not the only person raising capital out there. What were other people doing in my industry that I could duplicate? You know, Copy Your Way To Success. Who could I find that would personally guide me?

The local REIA (Real Estate Investor Associations) had lots of big-time players doing lots of deals, so I started looking there. I reached out to my sphere of people and started asking that question. Again, copy your way to success. People shared with me all kinds of stories and ways they had been raising capital. I only interviewed people I knew who were killing it and doing really big things. I did not waste my time asking people who were not top-level players. It wasn't long before I figured out what I needed.

It seemed everyone I talked to had a Private Money Program and a Credibility Kit.

PRIVATE MONEY PROGRAM

So what's a Private Money Program? It's a fancy way of saying I have a written down version of how people give me their money. I show them what to expect, the process, how I pay their money back, how it's secured, etc. It's basically what investors can expect if they give me their money. I found everyone operating at a high level had a version of this.

More importantly, a Private Money Program allows you to distinguish yourself as a professional. My first guide was crude and not very polished.

Over time, I came to realize the more I was thoughtful in putting together this document, meaning nicer graphics, better layout, presentation, the more people started to self-select. People looked at your presentation and started telling themselves whether you seemed credible or not.

The guide was a foreign concept at first because I always thought people with money always made the rules. What I found is that is quite the opposite. People with money have money problems. They need to make their money grow. Most want to be good stewards of their money, and when they hear of new opportunities, they will listen. They will be open to your proven process and will abide by your terms to get the yield they are looking for.

Now, this doesn't work for big banks, large investors, hedge funds, or family office lenders. They all have their rules 99 percent of the time. These types of lenders have a business that follows a set of guidelines on how they lend, what the interest rates are and how much they will lend to you. It's called LTV (Loan to Value). They also dictate the points you will pay, when you will make your payment if it's interest only, etc. These big businesses set the rules.

But, I wasn't looking at big businesses. I worked with people like Carl.

Big Idea:

Most people think Hard Money Lenders are the only ones lending Fix-n-Flip Money!

I learned a valuable lesson when it comes to capital. I call this now your Avatar. I look for investors who are investing in the stock market. This is the majority of people out there. They have IRAs and are not getting great returns. We can help these people greatly without competition.

I knew my investments made sense, and I knew there were people out there looking for me, a deal maker. You see, I feel no one trusts the stock market anymore, especially after the last crash.

You give your money to a stockbroker. Do you think he pays attention? He invests it based on your risk tolerance and time horizon, but after that, they don't have much control.

I'm beating up financial advisors here, and I want to say I have no ill will against them. In fact, there are a lot of good advisors out there. More and more I think the industry is coming to more of an advisory role. I think this is a much better option than paying an upfront sales load or commission.

My real issue with most companies in the financial world is that they do not offer real estate. The main reason for this is that real estate is ill-liquid. Meaning, you cannot trade in and cash out quickly like you can in stocks, bond, and mutual funds.

It is for this reason most financial institutions do not offer real estate. Because they don't offer it, most advisors cannot advise you to purchase real estate. Instead, most will offer a REIT. The problem with that is they are still selling a paper asset.

I've found most people want to invest in real estate. Unfortunately, most do not have the time needed to become a professional. They know that most wealthy people own real estate and they know they can profit from it. They can't seem to get there.

This, my friends, is where the opportunity is. You get good at real estate, and then we get to help people make money.

People, and I mean millions of people, are out there looking for this solution. They want an alternative to stock, bonds, and mutual funds. You see, they are looking for us.

What can a Private Money Program do for you?

First, it dictates how people should expect to work with you. For example, I only wanted to pay 12 percent interest when I first started. I didn't want to make monthly payments, and I wanted 100 percent of purchase price plus the cost to fix up the deals I did.

So, in my program, it states just that.

When we have deals we offer to an investor, the interest rate is 12 percent, interest only, and I only pay off the note when I sell it. The interest is accrued. Why? Because in my program, it details out how that works. I have a really detailed FAQ page that goes over everything. My program contains all the questions most investors have.

Next, you can explain to potential investors where a lot of their money is at that they didn't know they could use. We have a big section that talks about IRA and how people can use IRAs to invest. We give them places to reach out to so they can set it up the right way. The point is, people can use their IRA to invest in real estate.

Your guide can be as robust as you'd like it, but I find the simpler it is, the more people self-select. Remember this adage: A confused mind says NO!

With this new tool, I could now send potential investors an email with my Program. Whether they read it or not didn't matter. The fact that I had a Program put me a notch above everyone else. It made me look better, yet it made me feel professional.

So now I have confidence. I have a Private Money Program, but something was still missing. The number one question I was getting asked by investors was about my experience. They were questioning how many deals had I done, etc. At this point, in my head, I knew I had done quite a few wholesale deals, some 50/50 deals with Bob, and I had my deal with Carl and a few others. I didn't have any of this on paper.

That's when I created my first Credibility Kit.

Big Idea:

Document every deal you do, use pictures, video, tell a story. One day you will look back and be glad you did.

Bob Norton taught me how to use video when I was doing 50/50 deals with him. I never stopped. Looking back, this has helped propel my business, and the videos tell a compelling story. I was a real estate professional.

I hope you can see the benefit of creating a Private Money Program, and if you're doing fix-n-flips, it's a must. I want to give you my guide I have used for free as a gift for making it this far into the book. If you'd like my Private Money Guide text the word: **COPY** to **480-500-1127.**

The next big thing that will help you raise a crap ton of private capital in a single-family deal is a Credibility Kit.

Credibility Kit

As I began telling my story in my Private Money Program to potential investors, I found it helped if I could show them what I had done.

A Credibility Kit is a summary of your experience. You should use this to show your ability or demonstrate your expertise. Luckily for me, I had video and pictures of every deal I did, even the ones that I wholesaled to my investors where I did all the work, and they made all the money. Thank you, Bob . . .

So all I did was take the videos of me going into crappy homes, then the pictures of the deals fixed up and sold on the MLS and put them in a document I now call The Credibility Kit.

I also included my power team and all the professional contacts I used to do my single-family fix-n- flip business. You can get my Credibility Kit as well by texting **COPY** to **480-500-1127.** I think you will find it very useful, and you will be able to click some of my YouTube links to see me putting into practice everything I've said up to this point.

I hope you see this is not rocket science thus far. I feel like most all the things I talk about and do are very common sense. That leads me to my next big idea.

Big Idea:

Don't be a maverick. Be willing to listen and ask questions. Find things that are working and model them in your business.

All my biggest leaps in real estate have come from learning a skill from someone else. I have never been that smart. But, I guess one could argue that because I take this approach, I'm smart beyond measure. I've always valued learning from people better than me.

I had plenty of confidence, the Private Money Program, and my Credibility Kit, and I went out and started crushing it. I talked with anyone who would listen, and using my technique, only the right people self-selected. Before long, I had around three million dollars constantly working in my fix n flip business.

Now, I could stop this story right here, and you would be thinking wow, Corey, you made it. You started from nothing, and now you're doing lots of deals, and you're a success. Because when we turn on the TV, we turn on Flip This House, and we see people who are doing these deals, and they always make a ton of money and are living the life.

I'm not going to lie, I was in a way better spot than before when I had lost my job, but I need your absolute attention 'cause I'm about to drop some truth bombs.

In the world's eyes, I was a success. I had achieved and was operating at a high level. I was flipping three to six homes every month, and I was literally doing it all by myself.

If you pay attention to anything in this book, please hear me now, because I almost lost everything dear to me.

This next chapter represents a dark period in my life that shaped my future.

THE COST OF SUCCESS

I N 2008-2011 I WAS using two to three million dollars of OPM (Other People's Money) on a regular basis to fund my real estate acquisitions. I found sharing my story, asking people who they knew, having them self-select themselves was so rewarding. More importantly, I was doing real estate big time.

I was starting to realize my dreams and goals. The wife was proud. Things were going really, really good, but I didn't know my ship was sailing to risky waters and the price I would have to pay.

It started off as ,"Hey, honey, I've got to work a little tonight. You go on and go to bed." But, before

I knew it, I was a full-blown workaholic. My phone and I were always available to do deals on any day at any time.

I never put my phone down. I would show up to my kid's practice and be on it. I'd go to events to learn new things in real estate only to go into the hallway to make calls and take care of business.

I was not running my business. My business was running me.

I didn't see it at the time, but I was becoming irritable and short-tempered with my wife, the woman I worshipped most in life. Most of the time I was checked out. I was focused on the next deal. You see, I had a number in my head. If I can just get to this number, then I could take my foot off the gas.

I justified my actions and told myself that I was sacrificing for my family and that it would all pay off.

In reality, I couldn't have been farther from the truth.

Here's the truth, and I want you to listen up.

If I were to ask a room full of single-family fix-n-flippers or wholesalers in private how their real estate business was doing and to be honest with me, they would tell me that they were tired of the Hustle 'n Grind. What they wouldn't want to tell me is that they weren't sure if they were making money. What they would never tell me was that their life was a wreck and they were about to lose their wife and family because they were a complete mess.

Hustle 'N Grind

The hustle 'n grind is real. Most of us never stop. I was no exception. I put my foot on the gas and go full out. Here's the problem with that. I never took the time to work on my business to develop systems. My day started with finding deals, analyzing these deals, making offers, getting private money lined up, then jump in my truck to drive to my properties under construction.

I'd arrive at a property and be totally upset to find my subs were doing things wrong, or that I had made a mistake and did not order all the parts needed. Next thing you know, I was off to Home Depot or Lowe's to become a professional parts runner. This was my life every day. Little by little I was becoming more agitated, and my temper became shorter and shorter. I was burning out.

What You Would Not Want to Tell Me

On TV, every house they sell always seems to be perfect and make a crap ton of money.

Here's the reality.

It's not always sunsets and palm trees.

Sometimes life gives you deals to test what you're made of. These are the deals you lose money on. These are the deals that never made production on TV. They somehow got left on the editing floor. But for anyone who has been in this business for a while, you will have deals you will lose money on.

Something will happen. The market will become soft. You will underestimate the cost of rehab. You name it, a million things can happen.

In an attempt to do more volume and make more money, what seems to happen for a lot of investors is they have no idea where they are.

There were times in my single-family fix-n flip days when I played this game called move the money. Closing on a deal here, wiring money there, all while hoping and praying that the deal actually closes because you need those funds.

This struggle is all too real for a lot of investors. It's not as pretty as most people will tell you. Now, don't get me wrong, it's not like I didn't make any money. But, I was on a hamster wheel.

What's worse is what you wouldn't tell me.

What You Would Never Tell Me

It's one thing to lose money; it's an entirely different thing to lose your family. I've met too many real estate investors who share this story. With the goal to create wealth, they decided not to give their family the time it needed and craved.

What most investors would never tell me is that their home life is a wreck and they are on the verge of a divorce or losing it all.

This leads me to my story.

In the quest to make money, I lost focus on what's the most important thing. One Friday night before my son's soccer game scheduled for 3:00 p.m. Saturday, my son is lying on me on the couch, and we are talking. He turns around and looks into my eyes with love, and says, "Dad, are you going to be at my game tomorrow?"

I had set the expectation with my kids that sometimes Daddy has to work, and most of the times I was at games, but sometimes I would have to miss.

By my son asking me, it meant he wanted me

there. I looked back into my son's eyes and told him, "Yes. I will be there. You can count on me."

He then snuggled into my arms as I stroked the back of his hair and showed him my affection. I was so proud of the man my son was becoming. He gave his all in his sports and was still maintaining good grades. I was a proud dad.

As I sat there with my son, I started to formulate my plan. You see, I had missed three houses that week and had not checked up on them. I needed to check on the progress and make sure the rehab was being done and that the timeline was working at these properties. In my mind, I had to do this. I told myself, I'd wake up early and get that work done and be at the fields at 3:00 to see my son play.

The next morning, I rose up early just like I planned. When I arrived at the first job site, it immediately turned into a mess. The tile guys where laying tile, but they were laying it wrong. That led to me blowing up and getting upset. Also, Lowe's had forgotten to load some sinks and faucets, and my plumber was there, and he didn't want to have to come back. Wanting the job to get completed, I hurried off to Lowe's to pick up the parts and return as quickly as possible.

I get back to the house, and I'm starting to feel it

inside. I'm running late. I need to turn this around. I rush and speed to the next job and run into more problems. I ended up spending more time than expected at that site.

I still think I can make it.

The only problem is that the next job site is across town. I race to it and get that job inspected.

I then take a look at my watch. I have thirty minutes to get to my son's game. The only problem is that it takes forty-five minutes from where I am at.

Along the freeway on the way to my son's game, there was a huge wreck. Long story short, I show up to the game as it ends.

If you're a dad and you're reading this right now and you're doing this business, I want you to feel my pain. Let it sit in your heart for a minute so you will never have to experience it as I did.

I make it to the sidelines. The game is over, and my son is walking with his mom. I get there, and I'm trying to be positive, but then my son and I lock eyes, and I can see him trying to hide his disappointment in me. He's trying to hold it back, but then a tear starts to fall from his eye followed by a flowing stream. My son then looks at me and says, "Dad, you promised."

He's trying to hold it in as he's struggling with

his breathing. I pull his head in my heart, and then he loses it and sobs uncontrollably in my chest as I follow suit.

His little heart is shattered, and at that moment, I feel like a total and complete failure. The pain of disappointing a young heart that loves you more than life itself is one I hope you never experience.

As I'm rocking my son whose head is buried in my chest, all I can tell him is "I'm sorry." I repeat it over and over again, stroking the back of his head, feeling like the worst father ever.

We walk back to my truck, and he jumps in and together we drive home. My son quietly sniffles and sobs as he's visibly trying to calm down. No words are said, but no words are needed.

My son still loves me, and by him riding in my truck and not with Mom was a way of him saying "I forgive you." But, I knew something had to change, and it had to change immediately.

I couldn't believe myself. Was this what I had become, a father who disappoints his kids? Emotionally, I felt like a failure.

I asked myself, why?

Why did I choose looking at those homes instead of being present? My dad worked out of town for his job, but the one person I could count on when

I was young and up to high school was my grand-pa. He never missed. I loved knowing that he was watching. My grandpa was always there after the game giving me an attaboy and telling me how he loved a play or the way I did something. It meant so much to me and yet, I was not giving this to my own son, and I knew those kind words coming from my grandpa meant a lot to me. Seeing the disappoint-ment in his eyes is what really broke me.

When we got home, my wife looked at me. It was that look that things need to change. She has always supported me, but what I was doing was af-fecting my entire family. I told her I needed some time to myself, and I jumped in my truck and went for a drive.

While driving, I was reflecting on everything I had done. How did I go from a full-time dad, one who had been there for my kids every move, to one that made a promise and did not keep it?

My son looked up to me, but if I continued down this path, what was I headed for? How would he judge me? I also went back to Hawaii in my mind and thought about the vision I had. Bruce had shown me the perfect vision of time and money. I was starting to make money, but the cost was no longer worth it.

While driving endlessly, I kept on asking myself, why? Why did I have to look at those homes? Why did I break my son's heart? Why did I feel like a fraud? I started to fall in deep despair. Was real estate the right vehicle? Who was I becoming? Why did I feel so ashamed? Would he truly forgive me? Although I was alone, I could feel him crying in my arms. I could feel his body shake as he just let it all out. I punished myself in my mind. I was angry with myself. I screamed at myself, telling myself you're a $%&*ing idiot. Why did you do that?

I tormented myself until my eyes were red. I felt exhausted and overwhelmed with emotion. It was in my deepest and darkest hour beating myself up driving alone in my truck feeling like a complete failure as I cried out loud in gut-wrenching agony to God asking for his forgiveness. Family had been the cornerstone of my "why," and I had flung it out the window for the love of money. This was not the way, and I knew if I continued down this path, I would lose everything I held dear.

As I sobbed to myself replaying the look in my son's eyes over and over, a calmness started to fall over me eventually. I had finally accepted the fact I screwed up. I talked with God while driving mindlessly around town. It took a while, but I finally forgave myself.

In that calmness of clearing my mind and allowing it not to beat myself up, I knew I wanted to solve my problem. And then it happened.

On my way home, I drove past an apartment complex. I'd driven past this apartment complex a million times.

I would always say to myself, "I wish I could own an apartment." That was all it was. It was just a wish. But that day, in my broken state, clear and calm headed, I drove past the apartment complex, but this time I did something that I forgot I used to do. I asked myself a simple question. I said to myself, "How can I own an apartment complex?"

That simple question changed my life forever because, at that moment, I gave myself a "solve for X" type of Algebra problem. Before I knew I was even doing it, I found myself asking more questions.

My first question was, what do I know about buying an apartment complex? I told myself not a whole lot. I then asked the question, if I wanted to find out how to buy an apartment, where would I find that kind of information? Where could I possibly learn from someone who had done what I wanted to do?

My brain was firing on all cylinders now. I told myself, I knew I could find information on multi-family at Barnes & Noble. Next thing I know, I'm whipping my truck around in a U-turn and heading to the bookstore. I bought five books that night on apartments.

Somehow, my brain had subconsciously remembered Bruce had owned apartments. He was not doing fix-n-flip or wholesale. He had owned cash-flowing apartment complexes.

I drove home confidently that night back to my loving home. I went to the backyard with my wife and told her I was sorry and gave her my new vision. And like the ride or die wife she is, she took me into her arms and said, "Honey, I believe in you. I know you will fix this."

Big Idea:

If you are doing Fix-n-Flip or Wholesale, you are a TRADER, but if you do it long enough you will feel like a TRAITOR!

Robert Kiyosaki never once talked about fix-n- flip or wholesale. He talked about cash flow. Most who have read his book fell in love with that concept. We wanted to be investors in real estate, but something happened.

What happened is we turned on the stupid TV and watched a show called Flip This House. Somehow our minds became brainwashed, as we traded cash flow for quick profits.

Here's the truth about fix-n-flip and wholesale. The more you make, the more you pay in taxes. You are virtually self-employed.

Now, I understand some have a fully functioning business that has all the systems and run great, and it's a process. I want to remind you, the ESBI quadrants have four spots. "E" stands for Employee. This is someone who has a job and works that job. "S" stands for Self-Employed. These are people who own their job, like doctors, dentists, chiropractors. If they are not there doing the work, they don't get paid. "B" stands for Business. When you have a business, it usually has systems that allow your business to run without you and it can generate good amounts of income. "I" stands for Investor. Usually, when you have a "B" or Business and you make good income, you invest that money to where you are an I, or an Investor. "I" is where you have passive income coming in that you do not work for.

A business is not the end goal, the true investor is. The "I" category is the place you want to be. It's where the magic happens. When you can get paid time and time again because your money is working for you, it's a beautiful thing.

I took those five books home, and I knew I would find a new way, a new answer to my dreams and goals. It felt different this time. I knew for certain I was on the right track. I knew this path absolutely led to what I call now the CashFlow Life; sunsets and palm trees on your terms.

Everything I had achieved up to this point was needed to learn. I had to have the experience with my son. I needed to understand the pain. It's like I tell my son with wrestling. We either win, or we learn. I was back in learning mode, but I was so much more powerful now. I knew I had, as Tony Robbins would call it, Personal Power. I knew my thoughts and dreams were like a nuclear power plant, possessing an enormous amount of potential energy.

Not only were my thoughts and dreams powerful, but when you focus the mind, it can harness that energy and allow you to do more than you ever knew possible.

I read all five books, and as Murphy's Law goes, the one that I connected with most was the last one I read. I read *Multi-Family Millions* by David Lindahl. This is another book that changed my life forever

It's crazy how adversity can motivate you. I think back to this time in my life, and I was HUNGRY . . . I had a burning desire to change my life to the one I wanted. The timing couldn't have been better. It was getting harder and harder to find fix-n-flip deals in my market. I was ready to go big.

My only problem now was finding a deal . . .

THE COREYLEONE METHOD

IT TOOK AN ENTIRE year of learning multi-family before I was comfortable enough to venture out and get it on. I was getting on brokers' lists in the areas I wanted. This allowed me to get the deal flow and start my underwriting process. You see, in most markets, real estate brokers control the supply of deals that come on the market. If you subscribe to these lists, you then can analyze those deals to see if they make sense to buy. I was able to look at potential deals. My issue was it was taking longer than I wanted.

I was networking like crazy at lots of multi-family events where there were hundreds of investors. Every time I went to an event, I was trying to find a deal. It wasn't working out. It seemed everyone I talked to was only looking for money and didn't want to give up much percentage of a deal out for a new person like me.

This was starting to frustrate me. After a lot of failures, I knew something had to change. I knew I had a lot of Private Money behind me and I knew I could act fairly quickly with it. That's when I formulated a new master plan.

On the next event, it was like the universe opened up and granted my wishes. On that day, I was sitting in the back of the room. The event was a little smaller than most I had been going to, close to 100-125 people in the room.

I can't remember who was speaking, but at the end of the first segment of a three-day event, the speaker asked if anyone had any announcements, etc.

This was my cue. It had magically appeared on day one early morning, and I was sitting at the back of the room. I immediately stood up from the back and raised my hand. The speaker called on me, and as he did, everyone turned around in their seat and all eyes were upon me.

I cleared my throat, then in a loud confident voice said, "My name is Corey Peterson, I have a

CRAP TON of money, and I'm looking for some deals. Are there any deals out there? If so, please come talk to me."

That week I didn't pay for lunch or dinner for the rest of the event. It was crazy. Everyone was pitching their deals to me and asking me to partner with them.

It was at that moment I learned something I now call the **Coreyleone Method**. It was as if I was the Godfather. You see, the money is always patient, the money always negotiates out of strength, the money always gets the last look. I used to think the money was in real estate, but I have come to realize, the money is in the MONEY.

When I put myself out there as someone who had or controlled capital and let everyone know I had it, it was magic. People lined up to pitch me, and I had the pick of the litter. I looked over all the deals that week. I believe I saw every deal at that event. It was indeed MAGIC.

I waited until the event was almost over and then I made my move. One group had approached me and was in desperate need of my capital. They had a deal under contract, but their earnest money was now hard. Better yet, they had two weeks to close and needed 1.4 million dollars to seal the deal and do needed repairs.

It was now time to test the Coreyleone Method. I got the group in a room, and then the negotiations began. I immediately shocked the crap out of them when I offered to do their deal and bring needed funds for 90 percent ownership of the project. They almost jumped out of their skin. But for me, I sat calm, cool and collected. I knew I had the money, and I knew it could act very quickly.

LEVERAGE

Understanding the power of leverage is sometimes underestimated. When you have it, it's awesome because you're negotiating from strength. Leverage comes in many shapes and forms. One constant lever that I know is the MONEY.

The money is what gave me the Coreyleone Method. It's the mindset of the Godfather. I choose who, when, what I want to do. I have no fear because when you know you can get money to fund deals, it allows you to cut the best deals.

This is why I teach people to find the money first and not find the deal.

After freaking everyone out with my 90 percent offer, we got down and dirty. They thought they were going to get a 50/50 by the look on their faces. I knew this was probably the case and is why I started so lopsided. I needed them to see who had leverage quickly.

The real leverage in this case was not my money. It was the thought of them losing their 100k earnest money that was now hard and at risk if they didn't close in two weeks.

I knew this, and when I explained the real situation to them, and they had to hear it from me, the big bad balloon started to deflate.

I ended up getting 75 percent ownership of that first deal. But we only had a verbal agreement. I was absolutely pleased with myself. All those years ago when I was selling used cars paid off big time. Now, I had to underwrite this thing and make sure it was as good as they were claiming, and I had to do it quick. We had two weeks till our closing date.

That's exactly what I did. We had a verbal agreement. I needed a week to inspect the property and to look over the financials. The full year I took mastering the process of underwriting was now in effect. I was so glad I didn't skip steps in learning the HOW TO.

By the end of the week, I knew this was not only going to be a good deal, but it was also going to crush it. The property was called Lion's Gate in Mauldin, South Carolina. The group I was partnering with had locked the property up for 3.2 million. It was 78 percent occupied and was in receivership with the bank. It was suffering from deferred maintenance and bad management. It also had a bad reputation. When you were on the property at night, you could see a lot of foot traffic and drug use on the property. In other words, this property looked and felt like money. I knew I had the skills to fix this property and make money.

What was crazy was this property was about three miles from all the big box stores, Lowe's, Home Depot, Target, etc. This was a C Class Property very close to an A area. The best mix possible. I knew my team could pull it together.

We rate apartments using a Grading Scale of ABCD. "A" equals the nice new built properties. "B" being properties built in the 80's and 90's. "C" is for the late 60's and 70's. "D" is just called the warzone. In my opinion, you should avoid this type of property. Also location is rated the same way. "A" equals great area. "D" equals warzone.

Once I knew this was a deal, my next step was to make sure we had a legal agreement with my new partners. I got my 75 percent in writing.

Now, we only had a week to get all the money together. It was now that I was feeling stressed. I needed more time to pull all the funds together. This property needed 1.4 Million dollars of private capital. After careful review of the contract, I found an easy clause to exercise. If I paid $50k, I could get a thirty-day extension, per the paperwork.

We got the extension so that we had breathing room, and thirty days later, I wired 1.4 Million dollars to the title company. I had finally done it; I just bought my first property.

Right here in my story is the part I smile at.

It took so much work to get to this spot. I had failed so many times. I had tried so many different strategies, I had lost money, I had made some money, but more importantly, I had never given up. It was a big day indeed, but the new work was starting on this project. I still had a lot to do in order to make this deal work. Buying it was just the first step.

Big Idea:
The Money is in the MONEY

Once you understand the velocity of money and what you can do when you get a lot of it together and point it in the right direction, you will want to do nothing else.

I just finished holding one of my teaching events called the Kahuna Boardroom, **www.KahunaBoardroom.com** and everyone was surprised when I told them how I think when it comes to finding a deal or finding the money first. My reply has always been the same.

Find the money.

Always seek capital first.

Anyone can find a deal. It's a very easy task and very much a process of elimination. Finding capital, however, is a much more refined process and it takes a lot more work to develop.

People tell me, "Corey, if you find a deal, the money comes." I will not disagree, but when that deal comes, the person with all the money will take the majority ownership and allow you to make a small fraction of that deal.

Responsibility to the Capital

The power of raising private money also comes with great responsibility. Just because you can raise lots of money doesn't mean you know how to make it grow. I've seen a lot of people do this business wrong and overpromise and underdeliver.

First, the industry is regulated by the Securities and Exchange Commission, the SEC, meaning there are do's and don'ts.

When you pool capital together, meaning multiple people in a deal, and the investors are passive, you are creating a security. There is a right way and a wrong way. Make sure you always seek legal counsel when creating a Private Placement Memorandum, a legal document needed for raising money.

I always say that raising capital and the power of telling a story can be used for good or evil. You have to decide for yourself what path you are going to take.

The path I recommend is to disclose everything fully and always treat your money like it's the goose that lays the golden eggs. Because guess what, that's exactly what your capital does for you. You need to protect your capital.

Protect your capital, what does that mean? In my opinion, it means you do not put it in harm's way. In other words, when you are looking at potential deals, you do an extreme amount of underwriting. More importantly, you are conservative. You don't look at a deal with the best outcome. You measure a deal with the worst possible outcome with the conservative outcome. Another way to say this is "DON'T SPEED." Take your time and underwrite only PHAT deals. If you don't have an underwriting tool, I strongly recommend getting mine.

It's called the Kahuna CashFlow Calculator. You can get it for only $197 dollars with all the training videos on how to underwrite multi-family apartments conservatively. Go to **www.Kahuna-CashFlowCalculator.com.**

DRUG PROBLEM SOLVED

ONCE I OWNED LION'S GATE, the real work followed. We needed to fix certain issues with the property, and we needed to fix them fast. The first thing we needed to fix was the people.

You see, most successful businesses come down to the people. The people running your company will make or break it. Not only the people running your company, but also the people you choose to do business with.

At Lion's Gate, we knew we had the wrong people running our apartment complex. We also knew we wanted to have better people living in them as well.

After having the current team in place for a week analyzing them, it was a clear and easy decision to let them go. They were not playing full out. They didn't own the responsibility of this property.

We make all our managers live on-site as well as the head of maintenance too. This is done for a reason. They cannot hide from it. They have to own what they are creating. Do you want crazy tenants living in your neighborhood? Neither do our staff.

Next thing we needed to fix was our drug problem. By watching the property at night, we had seen a lot of traffic in certain buildings, and we knew this was not good.

Step one was to hire a police officer to patrol the property at night. This was easy to do. We gave him his unit for free. In return, he walked the buildings at night and kept the peace. This seemed to fix a lot of the issues we were having. But, the next step fixed it for sure.

After talking with our officer and developing a great relationship with him, we focused on the troubled area of my complex. We both agreed drugs were coming and going from some of the units. We just weren't certain which one. Enter step two.

Step two was awesome.

In our discussion, I asked if the city had any drug dogs and would they like an opportunity to train. It just so happened I had a wonderful apartment complex with lots of space, and I knew how to get access to all the units.

On Friday morning we gave a 24-hour notice to all tenants that the Mauldin Police were going to conduct a drug search of all units. Would you believe in the middle of the night we had two move-outs?

Drug problem solved.

Because we fixed a big issue on our property, what happened next was icing on the cake. You see, most of the tenants in the bad area knew the problem and what unit it was in. But they would never rat someone out. Because we solved this problem, these tenants came into the leasing office singing our praise and expressed how thankful they were that we solved the drug problem.

Once we did this, it's crazy how the property started to turn around.

I owned this property for almost six years. Every year we were constantly improving the tenant quality. Every year we were slowly raising rents. We were creating a community making sure that our product would shine.

I had created a team of people to manage and watch over this property while I lived comfortably in my home in Phoenix, AZ. I loved calling all my investors sharing in the cash-flow profits we all enjoyed. If you want to learn about how to invest in our deals, go to **www.KahunaInvestments. com** and join our Kahuna Investor Membership. We have a process for you to get to know us, and for us to know you. Once we have established a substantive relationship, then you can get access to our new apartment deals to invest in.

Early in 2017, I felt like there was an opportunity to really cash in. Greeneville/Maulden, South Carolina was super hot. The growth of both towns was heating up, and I thought I could sell my property for a small fortune.

It turns out, I was right. In November of 2017, we sold Lion's Gate for $8.8 million dollars. After all the dust settled, we profited around $4.8 million dollars. Not bad for a country boy who grew up in West Plains, MO.

ce	Riverside Abstract	$	1,595.00	
	Greenville County	$	16,280.00	$ 16,280.00
	Commercial Due Diligence Services	$	4,550.00	
	NAI Earle Furman			$ 132,000.00
	Bell, Carrington Price & Gregg, LLC			$ 1,064.00
	Fox Rothschild LLP	$	10,000.00	
	Koss & Schonfeld, LLP	$	25,000.00	
	Alexander Forrest Investments, LLC			$ 176,000.00
	American Equity Exchange Inc.			$ 3,512.00
	Tinsley and Baker			$ 181,250.00
	Berger Harris LLP	$	3,540.00	
	Hammond Law LLC	$	1,510.87	
	Franklin Street	$	24,839.00	
	North Capital Private Securities Corporation	$	70,000.00	
sbursement	Cedar Grove Capital	$	4,176.42	
	Cedar Grove Capital	$	88,000.00	
	Graybill, Lansche & Vinzani, LLC	$	2,750.00	
		$	220,500.22	$ 3,952,667.06
		$	(388,294.30)	
QI for ACDC Holdings Group, LLC:				$ 4,847,332.94

But this is not the end of the story. What happens next is what has set me free for life.

We put the $4.8 Million profit with a 1031 exchange agent. This agent holds your profit in an account while you try and find another like-kind property. If you satisfy the exchange requirements, you can defer the taxes on all the profit you made of the sale. This means I got to put all $4.8 million in the next deal and defer tax.

That's exactly what I was able to do. I bought Eagle Village Apartments in Evansville, IN for $12.7 million dollars.

Follow me closely here 'cause it's about to get real. When we closed on this property, I took an acquisition fee of $381k, and the best thing about this property is that it will pay me around $450k per year as passive income. Look at this property.

Yes, just like that, one stupid deal I bought six years ago and sold turned into a new deal that has set me free for the rest of my life.

The best part is it's not the only one I own. I have various projects throughout the United States.

See this picture above? This is my "why." The woman in this picture did something magical for me. She believed when not many would. She had the courage to stick up for me and yet at times was the most-gentle woman I know when I failed miserably.

I truly owe all my success to her. I have a journal entry in our love book, and it says, "Honey, today is the day. Today is the day you no longer have to work again for the rest of your life. You let me take the risks. I've always known your love. Because you believed in me and trusted me, together we made sacrifices along the way, so that now we can live like no other."

Life is definitely different now, but in some ways not too much. I still live in the same house I bought in 2009. Although we could afford a much bigger house all decked out, our kids love our neighbors, and we do, too.

We have never put much stock in having money for money's sake. It's what you can do with the money that is important.

There's a scene in a movie that I love to talk about. Remember watching the movie *The Devil's Advocate* with Al Pacino and Keanu Reeves? Al Pacino plays the devil in this movie. In the movie, he's a kingpin, owning this big law firm and all the building surrounding his firm in New York. Keanu Reeves plays Kevin, a new ambitious lawyer in the firm who turns out to be the devil's son. In the scene I love, Al Pacino and Keanu are getting ready to go into the subway and ride the train. Al Pacino looks at Kevin, and in classic Al Pacino, says, "Kevin, the problem with you . . . is everyone sees you coming." The irony is that in this scene, Kevin looks like a sharp dressed to the T lawyer and Al Pacino looks just like everyone else riding the subway, yet Al Pacino is the one with all the money.

The reason why I like to tell this story is that I want to live my life being the one who doesn't have to showboat my success. I don't need or desire to have everyone know if I'm successful or not. I want to live my life and enjoy the people who matter most to me, my friends and my family.

Big Idea:
Play full out, have fun, stay humble.

Most people I know who have true wealth will surprise you. They don't always look it.

SUPPLIERS OF FUN

ONCE YOU ACHIEVE A certain amount of success, you have to find new ways to motivate you. In other words, you have to create new goals and new milestones, as a way of keeping score.

I equate this to climbing a mountain. How do you climb one? You start with a big goal. You say to yourself you want to get to the top, but to get there, you make smaller goals. Goals like, I need to go 20 feet. Once you get there, you say I want to go 20 more. You do this over and over until you reach the top.

Once you get to the top, it feels great. Reaching

a goal is so rewarding. But it's not on top that's so rewarding. It's knowing how you got to the top that means everything. I love this quote by Homer, "The Journey is the Reward."

This is truly the case in my journey. Looking back at all the adversity I have come through and all the things I had to figure out makes success feel so good.

I want to invite you to start your journey in multi-family. I invite you to do two things that I believe can get you into the CashFlow Life. First, I want you to start listening to my Podcast. It's called the Multi-Family Legacy Podcast. You can Google it to find it on iTunes. The next action you can take is to go to **www.KahunaWealthBuilders.com** and opt into my Quickstart Video Workshop series. In this video training, I show you how to find all the private money you will ever need and how to start getting deal flow from brokers across the country.

This is all FREE, my gift to you from me.

Now, with success comes responsibility. One of the things Shelley and I have come to realize is that we cannot fail to teach our kids the importance of money and to be humble.

For me, I'll never forget. I grew up on the other side of the pendulum. I remember going to Mc-

Donald's as a kid with my brothers and sisters. At a young age, I knew that I was not going to the counter and ordering. I knew I'd sit with my brothers and sisters, and we would get a hamburger and split our small fries. I remember having friends at McDonald's, and they were ordering Big Macs and Quarter Pounders. I remember going to my parents and whining saying why can't I have a Big Mac or Quarter Pounder, and then my folks had to teach me a lesson, but inside, I understood the pain in a way they felt.

It is in this I know I'm responsible for teaching my kids lessons in humility. My kids have it very different from when I grew up. When we vacation as a family, we go all out. There's not much that is off-limits. If they want something, if it's not crazy, we buy it or do it. It's amazing, and it's fun as all get-out.

However, when we are with others, a different thing happens. My kids are trained and know they cannot come to me with wanting this or that. Why? Because if my kids get something and it's in front of their friends, and then their parents can't do the same thing, it will make our neighbors feel like crap. Why would we ever want to subject our dearest friends we have come to love like that?

Yes, we have outgrown the neighborhood financially, but we are still here. We are here because we love our neighborhood and all the friends we have come to love and cherish. I know they are reading this now and I want to tell them all, they are the best. We have cherished the best bonds you could ever ask for. They are our support network. But, most of all, I call them all my dearest friends. I love you all.

This brings me to the reason of the title of this chapter, Suppliers Of Fun. After climbing my success mountain and getting to the top, I looked out and saw a new challenge, a new mountain to start climbing. I call this mountain, the Supplier of Fun. It is the reason Shelley and I work hard and keep score. We want to be able to do things with people we love and be able to treat them to things we have come to enjoy.

To supply the fun.

One way this has manifested is this fall. I'm taking my friends, my neighbors, we call the VEGAS 6, to Hawaii. I'm picking up the tab to stay eight days in a big house right on the beach. We are going to supply the fun, aka a sick house on the beach. We are also going to supply all the sick things we will do on the island. All they have to do is buy the plane tickets.

What's cool about this trip is that none of my

neighbors have been to Hawaii. This will go down as an epic trip, and we will have so much fun. It's my way of saying thank you for being great neighbors.

Isn't that fun? I sure think it is.

I truly hope you have enjoyed reading my book. I hope it has made you laugh, cry, and start believing in yourself. You see, I picked real estate, but you can pick anything you enjoy and love. The story is still the same. Find mentors, copy them, do what they do, and don't do what they don't do.

Once you do this long enough, one day you find you are the mentor, and you're still the student. You should always be learning and growing, but don't ever forget to reach below and pull someone up with you.

It's the reason I wrote this book. I want you to get inspired and find your passion. Stay curious, and don't ever quit. You can do amazing things. I know you can. Dream, and you can achieve it. Remember, your Paradise is Possible….

Big Idea:
Don't EVER QUIT.

Quitters never win, and winners never quit. You win, or you learn. Keep learning, and I promise you, you can achieve your wildest dreams.

MY GIFT TO YOU

I WANT TO LEAVE you with something to inspire you and get you fired up to take action. The best way I know how to do that is to tell a story. But, this is no ordinary story. This story is about my father and what he taught me as a young boy that has stuck with me my entire life. These three lessons have shaped me and made me the man I am today. I truly hope it touches you because it does me.

As a young boy of about four-years old, I worshipped my dad. I always wanted to be by his side. I looked up to him, and I thought he was a Greek GOD. At 6'2" with wild brown hair and a thick wild brown beard, my dad was a man's man. In my mind, he was a mountain man. He had thick, broad shoulders and bright blue eyes and was as tan as all getout.

My father was drafted by the Cleveland Indians right out of high school and was destined to play in the big leagues. He was a catcher and was very good. Unfortunately, someone took him out at home plate, and he had to have back surgery. Just like that, his career was over. But, he still had that athletic build.

When baseball didn't work out, my dad turned to roofing. My grandpa was a roofer, and so my dad learned the trade, and as a young boy at four years old, I wanted to learn the roofing business, too.

I wanted to be with my dad so bad that I begged him to take me with him to work. It's at that young age that this boy started turning into a young man.

At four-years old, I climbed up on the roof with my father. This is where my dad started giving me the master download on life and how it works.

Now, I'm not sure if anyone knows this, but roofing is hard work. Next to concrete, I think it's one of the hardest professions to take up. As a young boy, I was up for the task.

Dad and I climbed up the ladder to get on the roof. Dad pulls me aside and gets on his knee to look me straight in the eyes and says, "Son, this is going to be hard work today. But when you are faced with hard work, you make it a game. The game we are going to play today is who can bring their shingles up to the top of the ridge first."

You see, my dad and I were on one side, and there was another roofer shingling the other side. For me, that's all I needed. I had my marching orders. The goal was to race to the top. As a young boy, the job I had was to take the shingle bundles and break them up and unstick the shingles and lay them out for my father.

He would grab them, line each shingle up, then Bap, Bap, Bap, Bap as he would nail each shingle down with his pneumatic nail gun. There we were, father and son doing hard work and getting it done. I couldn't have been happier.

Of course, you know what happened. Dad and I were synced, and we crushed it. We got our shingles to the top first. We didn't win by just a little. We won by a lot.

But, what my father did next shaped me. You see, we could have sat there and basked in all the glory and celebrate. But my dad wasn't like that. Instead, what we did was jump on the other side and help the other roofer bring all his shingles to the top of the ridge.

Why did we do this?

Why did my father jump on the other side to help the other roofer?

Because you reap what you sow. Dad taught me this . He also taught me to be humble. Just because you best someone, doesn't make you any better than the next person.

BIG IDEA:

Make Hard Work A Game

When faced with a difficult task, make it a game. Keep score and play all out. Before you know it, you will look back and see how far you came.

Although my dad got injured in baseball, he never lost the love of the game. As my baseball coach, he would say to me, "Son, when you go up to bat, swing for the fences. Don't ever be ashamed of giving it your all and go big. But, son, more often than not, what will happen is you will strike out. When that happens, don't make a fuss. Grab your bat and start hustling back to the dugout. As you're running back, take a minute to look out of the corner of your eye and look that pitcher right in the eye. Then tell yourself, you may have got me this time, but I will get you next time."

Big Idea:
Swing For the Fences!

In life, go big. You will never regret giving your all and playing full out. Sure, there may be times that you fail. That's just part of the journey. Success wouldn't taste so sweet if there were no adversity.

The last thing my dad taught me was to HUS-TLE. Dad would say, "Corey, if a coach or anyone asks you to run around that tree or goal post, hustle. You should always want to be first. The only way you get beat is if someone physically beats you. Most of the time winning is mental."

I have always given my all in all that I've done. I don't think I had plain raw talent, but I was always hustling, and I could beat most people mentally.

In business, you have to HUSTLE. You have to put in some work in the beginning. The early bird gets the worm. It takes extreme focus and a never die attitude. Rocky Balboa said it best, "Let me tell you something you already know. The world ain't all sunshine and rainbows. It is a very mean and nasty place, and it will beat you to your knees and keep you there permanently if you let it. You, me or nobody is gonna hit as hard as life . . . until you *start believing in yourself, you ain't gonna have a life."*

Hustling is everything. It's a state of mind.

Big IDEA:

Hustle to make your dreams and goals come true.

If you have made it this far reading this book, you have what it takes. You are ready to start working toward the life you desire.

All my life, I have kept these three ideas close to my heart: make work a game, swing for the fences, and hustle in all that you do.

I hope you choose to keep them close to your heart as well. Life, liberty, and the pursuit of happiness is the American Dream. I'm living proof that the idea our country was founded upon is true. I look back upon my life and realize I was nothing special. I'm still that little boy who still dreams he can be or do anything he puts his mind to. I try to be the best me I can and help as many along the path.

I fear that I haven't left enough breadcrumbs behind for others to follow and see the path I took. I hope I have given enough examples and that you have become inspired.

As a final gift for making it to the end, I would like to give you one more thing. If you text the word: **GIFT to 480-500-1127** I will give you my Private Money Training for free. I sell this for $597. This training is a complete guide and an online membership site. It will show you how to find lots of private money with a step-by-step guide on the process.

Be bold, be strong, and believe in your heart that you deserve nothing but the best.

It all starts with a dream.

Your Paradise is Possible!

GLOSSARY

Real cstate investors will find this glossary helpful in understanding words and terms used in real estate transactions. However, some factors may affect these definitions. Terms are defined as they are commonly understood in the mortgage and real estate industry. The same terms may have different meanings in another context. The definitions are intentionally general, nontechnical, and short. They do not encompass all possible meanings or nuances that a term may acquire in legal use. State laws, as well as custom and use in various states or regions of the country, may in fact modify or completely change the meanings of certain defined terms. Before signing any documents or depositing any money preparatory to entering into a real estate contract, the purchaser should consult with an attorney to ensure that his or her rights are properly protected.

Abstract of Title: A summary of the public records relating to the title to a particular piece of land. An attorney or title insurance company reviews an abstract of title to determine whether there are any title defects that must be cleared before a buyer can purchase clear, marketable, and insurable title.

Acceleration Clause: Condition in a mortgage that may require the balance of the loan to become due immediately in the event regular mortgage payments are not made or for breach of other conditions of the mortgage.

Ad Valorem: Designates an assessment of taxes against property in a literal sense according to its value.

Adjustable Rate Mortgage Loans (ARM): Loans with interest rates that are adjusted periodically based on changes in a preselected index. As a result, the interest rate on your loan and the monthly payment will rise and fall with increases and decreases in overall interest rates. These mortgage loans must specify how their interest rate changes, usually in terms of a relation to a national index such as (but not always) Treasury bill rates. If interest rates rise, your monthly payments will rise. An interest rate cap limits the amount by which the interest rate can change; look for this feature when you consider an ARM loan.

Adverse Possession: A possession that is inconsistent with the right of possession and title of the true owner. It is the actual, open, notorious, exclusive, continuous, and hostile occupation and possession of the land of another under a claim of right or under color of title.

Agency: The relationship that exists by contract whereby one-person is authorized to represent and act on behalf of another person in various business trans- actions.

Agreement of Sale: Known by various names, such as contract of purchase, purchase agreement, or sales agreement, according to location or jurisdiction. A contract in which a seller agrees to sell and a buyer agrees to buy, under certain specific terms and conditions spelled out in writing and signed by both parties.

Amortization: A payment plan that enables the borrower to reduce a debt gradually through monthly payments of principal, thereby liquidating or extinguishing the obligation through a series of installments.

Annual Compounding: The arithmetic process of determining the final value of a cash flow or series of cash flows when interest is added once a year.

Annual Percentage Rate (APR): The cost of credit expressed as a yearly rate. The annual percentage rate is often not the same as the interest rate. It is a percentage that results from an equation considering the amount financed, the finance charges, and the term of the loan.

Appraisal: An expert judgment or estimate of the quality or value of real estate as of a given date. The process through which conclusions of property value are obtained. It is also referring to the formalized report that sets forth the estimate and conclusion of value.

Appurtenance: That which belongs to something else. In real estate law, an appurtenance is a right, privilege, or improvement, which passes as an incident to the land, such as a right of way.

Assessed Value: An official valuation of property most often used for tax purposes.

Assignment: The method or manner by which a right, a specialty, or contract is transferred from one person to another.

Assumption of Mortgage: An obligation undertaken by the purchaser of property to be personally liable for payment of an existing mortgage. In an assumption, the purchaser is substituted for the original mortgagor in the mortgage instrument and the original mortgagor is to be released from further liability in the assumption. The mortgagee's consent is usually required.

The original mortgagor should always obtain a written release from further liability to be fully released under the assumption. Failure to obtain such a release renders the original mortgagor liable if the person assuming the mortgage fails to make the monthly payments.

An assumption of mortgage is often confused with 'purchasing subject to a mortgage.' When one purchases subject to a mortgage, the purchaser agrees to make the monthly mortgage payments on an existing mortgage, but the original mortgagor remains personally liable if the purchaser fails to make the monthly payments. Since the original mortgagor remains liable in the event of default, the mortgagee's consent is not required for a sale subject to a mortgage.

Both assumption of mortgage and purchasing subject to a mortgage are used to finance the sale of property. They may also be used when a mortgagor is in financial difficulty and desires to sell the property to avoid foreclosure.

Balance Statement: A statement of the firm's financial position at a specific point in time.

Balloon Mortgage: Balloon mortgage loans are short-term fixed-rate loans with fixed monthly payments for a set number of years followed by one large final balloon payment ("the balloon") for the remainder of the principal. Typically, the balloon payment may be due at the end of 5, 7, or 10 years. Borrowers with balloon loans may have the right to refinance the loan when the balloon payment is due, but the right to refinance is not guaranteed.

Bankruptcy: A proceeding in a federal court to relieve certain debts of a person or a business unable to pay its debts.

Bill of Sale: A written document or instrument that provides evidence of the transfer of right, title, and interest in personal property from one person to another.

Binder or Offer to Purchase: A preliminary agreement, secured by the payment of earnest money, between a buyer and seller as an offer to purchase real estate. A binder secures the right to purchase real estate upon agreed terms for a limited period of time. If the buyer decides not to purchase/is unable to purchase, the earnest money is forfeited unless the binder expressly provides that it is to be refunded.

Blanket Mortgage: A single mortgage that covers more than one piece of real estate. It is often used to purchase a large tract of land, which is later subdivided and sold as individual parcels.

Bona fide: Made in good faith; good, valid, without fraud; such as a *bona fide* offer.

Bond: Any obligation under seal. A real estate bond

is a written obligation, usually issued on security of a mortgage or deed of trust.

Breach: The breaking of law, or failure of a duty, either by omission or commission; the failure to perform, without legal excuse, any promise that forms a part or the whole of a contract.

Broker: One who is engaged for others in a negotiation for contacts relative to property, with the custody of which they have no concern.

Broker, Real Estate: Any person, partnership, association, or corporation who, for a compensation or valuable consideration, sells or offers for sale, buys or offers to buy, or negotiates the purchase or sale or exchange of real estate, or rents or offers to rent, any real estate or the improvements thereon for others.

Capital: Accumulated wealth; a portion of wealth set aside for the production of additional wealth; specifically, the funds belonging to the partners or shareholders of a business, invested with the express purpose and intent of remaining in the business to generate profits.

Capital Expenditures: Investments of cash or other property, or the creation of a liability in exchange for property to remain permanently in the business; usually pertaining to land, buildings, machinery, and equipment.

Capitalization: The act or process of converting or obtaining the present value of future incomes into current equivalent capital value; also, the amount so determined; commonly referring to the capital structure of a corporation or other such legal entity.

Cash Out: Any cash received when a new loan is obtained that is larger than the remaining balance of the current mortgage, based upon the equity already built up in the property. The cash out amount is calculated by subtracting the sum of the old loan and fees from the new mortgage loan.

Caveat Emptor: The phrase literally means "let the buyer beware." Under this doctrine, the buyer is duty bound to examine the property being purchased and assumes conditions that are readily ascertainable upon view.

Certificate of Title: A certificate issued by a title company or a written opinion rendered by an attorney that the seller has good marketable and insurable title to the property offered for sale. A certificate of title offers no protection against any hidden defects in the title that an examination of the records could not reveal. The issuer of a certificate of title is liable only for damages due to negligence. The protection offered a homeowner under a certificate of title is not as great as that offered in a title insurance policy.

Chain of Title: A history of conveyances and encumbrances affecting the title to a particular real property.

Chattel: Items of moveable personal property, such as animals, household furnishings, money, jewelry, motor vehicles, and all other items not permanently affixed to real property that can be transferred from one place to another.

Closing Costs: The numerous expenses that buyers and sellers normally incur to complete a transaction in the transfer of ownership of real estate. These costs are in addition to price of the property and are items prepaid at the closing day. The following is a common list of closing costs.

BUYER'S EXPENSES:

- Documentary Stamps on Notes
- Recording Deed and Mortgage
- Escrow Fees
- Attorney's Fee
- Title Insurance
- Appraisal and Inspection
- Survey Charge

SELLER'S EXPENSES:

- Cost of Abstract
- Documentary Stamps on Deed
- Real Estate Commission
- Recording Mortgage
- Survey Charge
- Escrow Fees
- Attorney's Fee

The agreement of sale negotiated previously between the buyer and the seller may state in writing who will pay each of the above costs.

Closing Day: The day on which the formalities of a real estate sale are concluded. The certificate of title, abstract, and deed are generally prepared for the closing by an attorney and this cost is charged to the buyer. The buyer signs the mortgage, and closing costs are paid. The final closing merely confirms the original agreement reached in the agreement of sale.

Cloud on Title: An outstanding claim or encumbrance that adversely affects the marketability of title.

Collateral Security: A separate obligation attached to a contract to guarantee its performance; the transfer of property or of other contracts or valuables to ensure the performance of a principal agreement or obligation.

Commission: Money paid to a real estate agent or broker by the seller as compensation for finding a buyer and completing the sale. Usually it is a percentage of the sale price ranging anywhere from 6 to 7 percent on single-family houses and 10 percent on land.

Compound Interest: Interest paid on the original principal of an indebtedness and also on the accrued and unpaid interest that has accumulated over time.

Condominium: Individual ownership of a dwelling unit and an individual interest in the common areas and facilities serving the multiunit project.

Consideration: Something of value, usually money, that is the inducement of a contract. Any right, interest, property, or benefit accruing to one party; any forbearance, detriment, loss or responsibility given, suffered or undertaken, may constitute a consideration that will sustain a contract.

Contract of Purchase: (See agreement of sale)

Conventional Mortgage: A mortgage loan not insured by HUD or guaranteed by the Veterans' Administration. It is subject to conditions established by the lending institution and state statutes. The mortgage rates may vary with different institutions and between states. (States have various interest limits.)

Cooperative Housing: An apartment building or a group of dwellings owned by a corporation, the stockholders of which are the residents of the dwellings. It is operated for their benefit by their elected board of directors. In a cooperative, the corporation or association owns title to the real estate. A resident purchases stock in the corporation, which entitles the resident to occupy a unit in the building or property owned by the cooperative. While the resident does not own the unit, the resident has an absolute right to occupy that unit for as long as he or she owns the stock.

Covenant: An agreement between two or more persons entered into by deed whereby one of the parties promises the performance of certain acts, or that a given state does or shall, or does not or shall not, exist.

Debt: An obligation to repay a specified amount at a specified time.

Debt Service: The portion of funds required to repay a financial obligation such as a mortgage, which includes interest and principal payments.

Deed: A formal written instrument by which title to real property is transferred from one owner to another. The deed should contain an accurate description of the property being conveyed, should be signed and witnessed according to the laws of the state where the property is located, and should be delivered to the purchaser on the day of closing. There are two parties to a deed—the grantor and the grantee. (See *also* deed of trust, general warranty deed, quitclaim deed, and special warranty deed.)

Deed of Trust: Just like a mortgage, a security instrument whereby real property is given as security for a debt; however, in a deed of trust there are three parties to the instrument—the borrower, the trustee, and the lender (or beneficiary). In such a transaction, the borrower transfers the legal title for the property to the trustee, who holds the property in trust as security for the payment of the debt to the lender or beneficiary. If the borrower pays the debt as agreed, the deed of trust becomes void. If, however, the borrower defaults in the payment of the debt, the trustee may sell the property at a public sale, under the terms of the deed of trust. In most juris- dictions where the deed of trust is in force, the borrower is subject to having the property sold without benefit of legal proceedings. A few states have begun in recent years to treat the deed of trust like a mortgage.

Default: Failure to make mortgage payments as agreed to in a commitment based on the terms and at the designated time set forth in the mortgage or deed of trust. It is the mortgagor's responsibility to remember the due date and send the payment prior to the due date, not after. Generally, 30 days after the due date if payment is not received, the mortgage is in default. In the event of default, the mortgagor may give the lender the right to accelerate payments, take possession and receive rents, and start foreclosure. Defaults may also come about by the failure to observe other conditions in the mortgage or deed of trust.

Depreciation: Decline in value of a house due to wear and tear, adverse changes in the neighborhood, or any other reason. The term is most often applied for tax purposes.

Down Payment: The amount of money to be paid by the purchaser to the seller upon the signing of the agreement of sale. The agreement of sale will refer to the down payment amount and will acknowledge receipt of the down payment. Down payment is the difference between the sales price and maximum mortgage amount. The down payment may not be refundable if the purchaser fails to buy the property without good cause. If the purchaser wants the down payment to be refundable, a clause in the agreement of sale should be inserted, specifying the conditions under which the deposit will be refunded, if the agreement does not already contain such clause. If the seller cannot deliver good title, the agreement of sale usually requires the seller to return the down payment and to pay interest and expenses incurred by the purchaser.

Duress: Unlawful constraint exercised upon a person, whereby the person is forced to perform some act, or to sign an instrument or document against his or her will.

Earnest Money: The deposit money given to the seller or the seller's agent by the potential buyer upon the signing of the agreement of sale to show serious intent about buying a house or any other type of real property. If the sale goes through, the earnest money is applied against the down payment. If the sale does not go through, the earnest money will be forfeited or lost unless the binder or offer to purchase expressly provides that it is refundable.

Easement Rights: A right-of-way granted to a person or company authorizing access to or over the owner's land. An electric company obtaining a right-of-way across private property is a common example.

Economic Life: The period over which a property may be profitably utilized or the period over which a property will yield a return on the investment, over and above the economic or ground rent due to its land.

Economic Obsolescence: Impairment of desirability or useful life arising from economic forces, such as changes in optimum land use, legislative enactments that restrict or impair property rights, and changes in supply and demand relationships.

Eminent Domain: The superior right of property subsisting in each and every sovereign state to take private property for public use upon the payment of just compensation. This power is often conferred upon public service corporations that perform quasi-public functions, such as providing public utilities. In every case, the owner whose property is taken must be justly compensated according to fair market values in the prevailing area.

Encroachment: An obstruction, building, or part of a building that intrudes beyond a legal boundary onto neighboring private or public land, or a building extending beyond the building line.

Encumbrance: A legal right or interest in land that affects a good or clear title, and diminishes the land's value. It can take numerous forms, such as zoning ordinances, easement rights, claims, mortgages, liens, charges, a pending legal action, unpaid taxes, or restrictive covenants. An encumbrance does not legally prevent transfer of the property to another. A title search is all that is usually done to reveal the existence of such encumbrances, and it is up to the buyer to determine whether to purchase with the encumbrance, or what can be done to remove it.

Equity: The value of a homeowner's unencumbered interest in real estate. Equity is computed by subtracting from the property's fair market value the total of the unpaid mortgage balance and any outstanding liens or other debts against the property. A homeowner's equity increases as the mortgage is paid off, or as the property appreciates in value. When the mortgage and all other debts against the property are paid in full, the homeowner has 100% equity in the property.

Escheat: The reverting of property to the state due to failure of persons legally entitled to hold, or when heirs capable of inheriting are lacking the ability to do so.

Escrow: Funds paid by one party to another (the escrow agent) to hold until the occurrence of a specified event, after which the funds are released to a designated individual. In FHA mortgage transactions, an escrow account usually refers to the funds a mortgagor pays the lender at the time of the periodic mortgage payments. The money is held in a trust fund, provided by the lender for the buyer. Such funds should be adequate to cover yearly anticipated expenditures for mortgage insurance premiums, taxes, hazard insurance premiums, and special assessments.

Estate: The degree, quantum, nature, and extent of

interest that one has in real property.

Execute*:* To perform what is required to give validity to a legal document. To exe cute a document, for example, means to sign it so that it becomes fully enforceable by law.

Fee Simple*:* The largest estate a person can have in real estate. Denotes totality of ownership, unlimited in point of time, as in perpetual.

Fiduciary*:* A person to whom property is entrusted; a trustee who holds, controls, or manages for another. A real estate agent is said to have a fiduciary responsibility and relationship with a client.

Foreclosure*:* A legal term applied to any of the various methods of enforcing payment of the debt secured by a mortgage, or deed of trust, by taking and selling the mortgaged property, and depriving the mortgagor of possession.

Forfeiture Clause*:* A clause in a lease enabling the landlord to terminate the lease and remove a tenant when the latter defaults in payment of rent or any

COREY PETERSON

other obligation under the lease.

Functional Obsolescence: An impairment of desirability of any property arising from its being out of date with respect to design and style, capacity and utility in relation to site, lack of modern facilities, and the like.

General Warranty Deed: A deed that conveys not only all the grantor's interests in and title to the property to the grantee, but also warrants that if the title is defective or has a "cloud" on it (such as mortgage claims, tax liens, title claims, judgments, or mechanic's liens against it) the grantee may hold the grantor liable.

Generally Accepted Accounting Principles (GAAP): A standardized set of accounting principles and concepts by which financial statements are prepared.

Grantee: That party in the deed who is the buyer or recipient; the person to whom the real estate is conveyed.

Grantor: That party in the deed who is the seller or giver; the person who conveys the real estate.

Hazard Insurance: Protects against damages caused to property by fire, wind- storms, and other common hazards.

Highest and Best Use: That use of, or program of utilization of, a site that will produce the maximum net land returns over the total period comprising the future; the optimum use for a site.

Implied Warranty or Covenant: A guaranty of assurance the law supplies in an agreement, even though the agreement itself does not express the guaranty or assurance.

Income Statement: The financial report that summarizes a business's performance over a specific period of time.

Injunction: A writ or order of the court to restrain one or more parties to a suit from committing an inequitable or unjust act regarding the rights of some other party in the suit or proceeding.

Interest: A charge paid for borrowing money.

Internal Rate of Return (IRR) Method: A method of ranking an investment proposal using the rate of return on an investment, calculated by finding the dis- count rate that equates the present value of future cash inflows to the project's cost.

Joint Tenancy: Property held by two or more persons together with the right of survivorship. While the doctrine of survivorship has been abolished with respect to most joint tenancies, the tenancy by the entirety retains the doctrine of survivorship in content.

Judgment: The decision or sentence of a court of law as the result of proceedings instituted therein for the redress of an injury. A judgment declaring that one individual is indebted to another individual when properly docketed creates a lien on the real property of the judgment debtor.

Lease: A species of contract, written or oral, between the owner of real estate, the landlord, and another person, the tenant, covering the conditions upon which the tenant may possess, occupy, and use the real estate.

Lessee*:* A person who leases property from another person, usually the landlord.

Lessor*:* The owner or person who rents or leases property to a tenant or lessee; the landlord.

Liabilities The debts of a business or entity in the form of financial claims on its assets.

LIBOR (London Interbank Offered Rate)*:* The interest rate charged among banks in the foreign market for short-term loans to one another. A common index for ARM loans.

Lien*:* A claim by one person on the property of another as security for money owed. Such claims may include obligations not met or satisfied, judgments, unpaid taxes, materials, or labor.

Limited Liability Partnership (Limited Liability

Company): A hybrid form of organization in which all partners enjoy limited liability for the business's debts. It combines the limited liability advantage of a corporation with the tax advantages of a partnership.

Limited Partnership: A hybrid form of organization consisting of general partners who have unlimited liability for the partnership's debts, and limited partners, whose liability is limited to the amount of their investment.

Loan Application: An initial statement of personal and financial information required to apply for a loan.

Loan Application Fee: Fee charged by a lender to cover the initial costs of processing a loan application. The fee may include the cost of obtaining a property appraisal, a credit report, and a lock-in fee or other closing costs incurred during the process, or the fee may be in addition to these charges.

Loan Origination Fee: Fee charged by a lender to cover administrative costs of processing a loan.

Loan-to-Value Ratio (LTV): The percentage of the loan amount to the appraised value (or the sales price, whichever is less) of the property.

Lock or Lock-In: A lender's guarantee of an interest rate for a set period of time. The period is usually that between loan application approval and loan closing. The lock-in protects you against rate increases during that time.

Market Value: The amount a property would sell for if put on the open market and sold in the manner property is ordinarily sold in the community in which the property is situated. The highest price estimated in terms of money that a buyer would be warranted in paying and a seller would be justified in accepting, provided both parties were fully informed, acted intelligently and voluntarily, and further-more that all the rights and benefits inherent in or attributable to the property were included in the transfer.

Marketable Title: A title that is free and clear of objectionable liens, clouds, or other title defects. A title that enables an owner to sell the property freely to others, and which others will accept without objection.

Meeting of Minds: A mutual intention of two persons to enter into a contract affecting their legal status based on agreed upon terms.

Metes and Bounds: A term that comes from the old English words "metes," meaning measurements, and "bounds," meaning boundaries. It is generally applied to any description of real estate; describes the boundaries by distance and angles.

Mortgage: A lien or claim against real property given by the buyer to the lender as security for money borrowed. Under government-insured or loan guarantee provisions, the payments may include escrow amounts covering taxes, hazard insurance, water charges, and special assessments. Mortgages generally run from 10 to 30 years, during which the loan is to be paid in full.

Mortgage Commitment: A written notice from the bank or other lending institution saying it will advance mortgage funds in a specified amount to enable a buyer to purchase a house.

Mortgage Note*:* A written agreement to repay a loan. The agreement is secured by a mortgage, serves as proof of an indebtedness, and states the manner in which it shall be paid. The note states the actual amount of the debt that the mortgage secures and renders the mortgagor personally responsible for repayment.

Mortgage (Open End)*:* A mortgage with a provision that permits borrowing additional money in the future without refinancing the loan or paying additional financing charges. Open-end provisions often limit such borrowing to no more than would raise the balance to the original loan figure.

Mortgagee*:* The lender in a mortgage agreement.

Mortgagor*:* The borrower in a mortgage agreement.

Net Cash Flow*:* The actual net cash, as opposed to accounting net income, that a firm generates during some specified period.

Net Income*:* In general, synonymous with net earnings, but considered a broader and better term; the balance remaining after deducting from the gross income all expenses, maintenance, taxes, and losses pertaining to operating properties except for interest or other financial charges on borrowed or other forms of capital.

Net Lease*:* A lease where, in addition to the rent stipulated, the lessee assumes payment of all property charges such as taxes, insurance, and maintenance.

Nonconforming Use*:* A use of land that predates zoning, but which is not in accordance with the uses prescribed for the area by the zoning ordinance. Because it was there first, it may be continued, subject to certain limitations.

Note*:* An instrument of credit given to attest a debt; a written promise to pay money, which may or may not accompany a mortgage or other security agreement.

Offer*:* A proposal, oral or written, to buy a piece of property at a specified price under specified terms and conditions.

Option*:* The exclusive right to purchase or lease a property at a stipulated price or rent within a specified period of time.

Percentage Lease*:* A lease of commercial property in which the rent is computed as a percentage of the receipts, either gross or net, from the business being con- ducted by the lessee, sometimes with a guaranteed minimum rental.

Personal Property*:* Moveable property that is not by definition real property, including tangible property such as moneys, goods, chattel, as well as debts and claims.

Planned Unit Development (PUD)*:* Residential complex of mixed housing types. Offers greater design flexibility than traditional developments. PUDs permit clustering of homes, sometimes not allowed under standard zoning ordinances, utilization of open space, and a project harmonious with the natural topography of the land.

Points*:* Sometimes referred to as 'discount points.'

A point is one percent of the amount of the mortgage loan. For example, if a loan is for $250,000, one point is $2,500. Points are charged by a lender to raise the yield on a loan at a time when money is tight, interest rates are high, and there is a legal limit to the interest rate that can be charged on a mortgage. Buyers are prohibited from paying points on HUD or Veterans' Administration guaranteed loans (sellers can pay them, how- ever). On a conventional mortgage, points may be paid by either buyer or seller or split between them.

Portfolio: The combined holdings of more than one stock, bond, real estate asset, or another asset by an investor.

Prepayment: Payment of mortgage loan, or part of it, before due date. Mortgage agreements often restrict the right of prepayment either by limiting the amount that can be prepaid in any one year or charging a penalty for prepayment. The Federal Housing Administration does not permit such restrictions in FHA insured mort- gages.

Principal: The basic element of the loan as distinguished from interest and mortgage insurance premium. In other words, principal is the amount upon which interest is paid. The word also means one who appoints an agent to act for, and in behalf of, the person bound by an agent's authorized contract.

Property*:* The term used to describe the rights and interests a person has in lands, chattel, and other determinate things.

Purchase Agreement*:* An offer to purchase that has been accepted by the seller and has become a binding contract.

Quiet Enjoyment*:* The right of an owner of an interest in land, whether an owner or a tenant, to protection against disturbance or interference with possession of the land.

Quitclaim Deed*:* A deed that transfers whatever interest the maker of the deed may have in the particular parcel of land. A quitclaim deed is often given to clear the title when the grantor's interest in a property is questionable. By accepting such a deed, the buyer assumes all the risks. Such a deed makes no warranties as to the title, but simply transfers to the buyer whatever interest the grantor has. (SEE deed.)

Real Estate Agent*:* An intermediary who buys and sells real estate for a company, firm, or individual and is compensated on a commission basis. The agent does not have title to the property, but generally represents the owner.

Real Estate Investment Trust (REIT)*:* An entity that allows a very large number of investors to participate in the purchase of real estate, but as passive investors. The investors do not buy directly, but instead purchase shares in the REIT that owns the real estate investment. REITs are fairly common with the advent of mutual funds and can be purchased for as little as $10 per share and sometimes less.

Real Property*:* Land and buildings and anything that may be permanently attached to them.

Recording*:* The placing of a copy of a document in the proper books in the office of the Register of Deeds so that a public record will be made of it.

Redemption*:* The right that an owner-mortgagor,

or one claiming under him or her, has after execution of the mortgage to recover back the title to the mortgaged property by paying the mortgage debt, plus interest and any other costs or penalties imposed, prior to the occurrence of a valid foreclosure. The payment discharges the mortgage and places the title back as it was at the time the mortgage was executed.

Refinancing: The process of the same mortgagor paying off one loan with the proceeds from another loan.

Reformation: The correction of a deed or other instrument by reason of a mutual mistake of the parties involved, or because of the mistake of one party caused by the fraud or inequitable conduct of the other party.

Release: The giving up or abandoning of a claim or right to the person against whom the claim exists or against whom the right is to be exercised or enforced.

Release of Lien: The discharge of certain property from the lien of a judgment, mortgage, or claim.

Renewal: Taking a new lease after an existing lease expires.

Rent: A compensation, either in money, provisions, chattel, or labor, received by the owner from a tenant for the occupancy of the premises.

Rescission of Contract: The abrogating or annulling of a contract; the revocation or repealing of a contract by mutual consent of the parties to the contract, or for other causes as recognized by law.

Restrictive Covenants: Private restrictions limiting the use of real property. Restrictive covenants are created by deed and may run with the land, thereby binding all subsequent purchasers of the land, or may be deemed personal and binding only between the original seller and buyer. The determination whether a covenant runs with the land or is personal is governed by the language of the covenant, the intent of the parties, and the law in the state where the land is situated. Restrictive covenants that run with the land are encumbrances and may affect the value and marketability of title. Restrictive covenants may limit the density of buildings per acre, regulate size, style, or price range of buildings to be erected, or prevent particular businesses from operating or minority groups from owning or occupying homes in a given area. This latter discriminatory covenant is unconstitutional and has been declared unenforceable by the U.S. Supreme Court.

Retained Earnings: That portion of a firm's earnings that has been saved rather than paid out as dividends.

Retained Earnings: That portion of the firm's earnings that has been saved rather than paid out as dividends.

Return on Assets (ROA): The ratio of net income to total assets.

Return on Equity (ROE): The ratio of net income to equity; measures the rate of return on common stockholders' investment.

Revocation: The recall of a power or authority conferred, or the vacating of an instrument previously made.

Right of Survivorship*:* Granted to two joint owners who purchase using that buying method. Stipulates that one gets full rights and becomes the sole owner of the property upon the death of the other. Right of survivorship is the fundamental difference between acquiring property as joint owners and as tenants in common.

Sales Agreement: (*SEE agreement of sale*)

Security Deposit*:* Money or things of value received by or for a property owner to ensure payment of rent and the satisfactory condition of the rented premises upon termination of the written or oral lease.

Security Interest*:* An interest in property that secures payment or performance of an obligation.

Special Assessment*:* A legal charge against real estate by a public authority to pay the cost of public improvements, such as for the opening, grading, and guttering of streets, the construction of sidewalks and sewers, or the installation of street lights or other such items to be used for public purposes.

Special Lien*:* A lien that binds a specified piece of property, unlike a usual or general lien, which is levied against all one's assets. It creates a right to retain something of value belonging to another person as compensation for labor, material, or money expended in that person's behalf. In some localities, it is called 'particular' lien or 'specific' lien. (SEE lien.)

Special Warranty Deed*:* A deed in which the grantor conveys title to the grantee and agrees to protect the grantee against title defects or claims asserted by the grantor and those persons whose right to assert a claim against the title arose during the period the grantor held title to the property. In a special warranty deed, the grantor guarantees to the grantee that nothing has been done during the time title to the property was held that has, or which might in the future, impair the grantee's title.

Specific Performance*:* A remedy in court of equity whereby the defendant may be compelled to do whatever was agreed to in a contract executed by the defendant.

Statute*:* A law established by the act of the legislative powers; an act of the legislature; the written will of the legislature solemnly expressed according to the forms necessary to constitute it as the law provides.

Subdivision: A tract of land divided into smaller parcels of land, or lots, usually for constructing new houses.

Sublease: An agreement whereby one person who has leased land from the owner rents out all or a portion of the premises for a period ending prior to the expiration of the original lease.

Subordination Clause: A clause in a mortgage or lease stating that one who has a prior claim or interest agrees that this interest or claim shall be secondary or sub- ordinate to a subsequent claim, encumbrance, or interest.

Survey: A map or plat made by a licensed surveyor showing the results of measuring the land with its elevations, improvements, boundaries, and its relationship to surrounding tracts of land. A survey is often required by the lender to assure that a building is actually sited on the land according to its legal description.

Survivorship: The distinguishing feature of a tenancy by the entirety, by which on the death of one spouse, the surviving spouse acquires full ownership.

Tax: As applied to real estate, an enforced charge imposed on persons, property, or income, to be used to support the State. The governing body in turn utilizes the funds in the best interest of the general public.

Tax Deed: A deed given where property has been purchased at public sale because of the owner's nonpayment of taxes.

Tax Sale: A sale of property for nonpayment of taxes assessed against it.

Tenancy at Will: An arrangement under which a tenant occupies land with the consent of the owner, but without a definite termination date and without any definite agreement for regular payment of rent.

Tenancy in Common: Style of ownership in which two or more persons purchase a property jointly, but with no right of survivorship. Each tenant in common is the owner of an undivided fractional interest in the whole property. They are free to will their share to anyone they choose, a primary difference between that form of ownership and joint tenancy.

Tenant: One who holds or possesses land or tenements by any kind of title, either in fee, for life, for years, or at will. The term is most commonly used as one who has under lease the temporary use and occupation of real property that belongs to another person or persons. The tenant is the lessee.

Time is of the Essence: A phrase meaning that time is of crucial value and vital importance and that failure to fulfill time deadlines will be considered a failure to perform the contract.

Title: As generally used, the rights of ownership and possession of a particular property. In real estate usage, title may refer to the instruments or documents by which a right of ownership is established (title documents), or it may refer to the ownership interest one has in the real estate.

Title Insurance: Protects lenders or homeowners against loss of their interest in property due to legal defects in title. Title insurance may be issued to a mortgagee's title policy. Insurance benefits will be paid only to the 'named insured' in the title policy, so it is important that an owner purchase an 'owner's title policy' if he or she desires the protection of title insurance.

Title Search or Examination: A check of the title records, generally at the local courthouse, to make sure the buyer is purchasing a house from the legal owner and there are no liens, overdue special assessments, or other claims or outstanding restrictive covenants filed in the record that would adversely affect the marketability or value of title.

Trust: A relationship under which one person, the trustee, holds legal title to property for the benefit of another person, the trust beneficiary.

Trustee: A party who is given legal responsibility to hold property in the best interest of or 'for the benefit of' another. The trustee is one placed in a position of responsibility for another, a responsibility enforceable in a court of law. (*See deed of trust.*)

Truth-in-lending Act: Federal law requiring written disclosure of the terms of a mortgage (including the APR and other charges) by a lender to a borrower after application. Also requires the right to rescission period.

Underwriting: In mortgage lending, the process of determining the risks involved in and establishing suitable terms and conditions for the loan.

Unimproved: As relating to land, vacant or lacking in essential appurtenant improvements required to serve a useful purpose.

Useful Life: The period over which a commercial property can be depreciated for tax purposes. A property's useful life is also referred to as its economic life.

Usury: Charging a higher rate of interest on a loan than is allowed by law.

Valid: Having force, or binding forces; legally sufficient and authorized by law.

Valuation*:* The act or process of estimating value; the amount of estimated value.

Value*:* Ability to command goods, including money, in exchange; the quantity of goods, including money, that should be commanded or received in exchange for the item valued. As applied to real estate, value is the present worth of all the rights to future benefits arising from ownership.

Variance*:* An exception to a zoning ordinance granted to meet certain specific needs, usually given on an individual case-by-case basis.

Void*:* That which is unenforceable; having no force or effect.

Waiver*:* Renunciation, disclaiming, or surrender of some claim, right, or prerogative.

Warranty Deed*:* A deed that transfers ownership of real property and in which the grantor guarantees that the title is free and clear of all encumbrances.

Zoning Ordinances: The acts of an authorized local government establishing building codes and setting forth regulations for property land usage.

WHY
THE RICH GET
RICHER

FOREWORD

by David Lindhal

I DISCOVERED THE POWER of multi-family apartments and cash flow over twenty-two years ago. As a seasoned operator of over 8,000 units across the country, you could say I've learned a thing or two. I have coached and mentored thousands of students in my life and it sometimes surprises me which students do and do not act along with the commitment required needed to succeed. After meeting Corey, though, I knew he would make it. Let me tell you a little story of what he did that confirmed this to me early in our relationship.

Corey had opted in and bought some of my online training courses and honestly, I did not know he existed. He participated in one of our live events and was ascending our value ladder with the education RE Mentor provides. Then, something unique happened. Corey had called the office and made it a requirement to have lunch with me if he was to enroll in our coaching program. This doesn't usually happen, and my first thought was Corey must be local or close to the Boston area where we are located. I asked Jeanie, my assistant, where this guy was from and what he wanted.

Jeanie replied that he was from Phoenix, AZ. I

thought to myself, well if I guy wants to fly all the way out here just to have lunch, I'll do it. I gave Jeanie a couple of dates that were open on my calendar a month away and went off with my day. In truth, I didn't have much faith that this would actually happen, but I wasn't going to say no.

Now my team is working my schedule, and we are about a week away from Corey's appointment. We'd not heard from him so I assumed he wasn't coming so we booked another meeting on top of his. I have Jeannie reach out, she comes back and says, "He's coming." And all I can say is, "Are you sure?"

Sure enough, Corey shows up on the day we're scheduled at my office ready to do lunch. Jeannie calls me once he comes in and says, "He's actually here. Looks like you're going to lunch." I quickly rearrange my schedule and off to lunch we go.

So, there I am talking with Corey about what he does and what his plans are since he'd never been to Boston. I am quickly surprised to find out that he's flying out later that evening. Then it hits me... He truly came all this way from Phoenix, AZ just to have lunch and meet me face to face!

I noticed something in Corey that reminded me a lot of myself. Corey was a doer. He didn't wait for things to happen - he made them happen. In fact, I find this gift shows up in most entrepreneurs. One must have a lot of guts, strength, passion, and strong belief in themselves to succeed. If entrepreneurship was easy, everyone would do it. I saw that look in Corey's eyes and I knew he would do it. Check out both our lunch meeting and in-office meeting at **https://youtu.be/wcMnTZzRXcA** and

WhyTheRichGetRicher.net/DavidLindahl

A year later, after completing my entire training system, Corey made things happen and purchased his first Multi-Family property – and many more followed. Corey has been on my stage and has encouraged others with his true rags to riches story. It's been a pleasure to watch him grow and succeed. I was very honored to be asked to write the foreword for this book and look forward to hearing many more of Corey's success stories. Check out a *How Did He Do That* from one of my events:

https://youtu.be/60oIcgL63sQ

David Lindhal

INTRODUCTION

DID YOU EVER PLAY Monopoly as a kid? I remember the games my family would play as we were growing up and how much fun we had. The rules were simple. Get a monopoly, build houses and then finally trade them in for hotels that charge the big bucks.

In my younger years, I didn't have a clue that in the future as a seasoned investor buying cash flowing, multi-family apartments, I would be playing monopoly in real life. Nor did I know I'd be making "the big bucks." I also didn't know the game I play now would be just as fun and exciting as back then. Finally, I didn't know the battle scars I'd endure from making mistakes along the way. If I have learned anything, it's that real estate is constantly changing. With the increase of technology, it's changing faster than ever. Not only is real estate changing, but how people want to make a living is changing as well.

I have sat across from hundreds of very high-income, successful people looking for ways to get out of the rat race. When I talk with these individuals, I hear many of the same things. Doctors, dentists, chiropractors and health care professionals are frustrated with health care being forced down their throats, all while seeing shrinking profit margins. They know if they don't go to work, they won't get paid. So, each day they go to work (like zombies), going through life yet not really living. I've seen business owners make huge profits, but then tell me how much they work and how unhappy they are. They want nothing more than to retire and enjoy life again. Then there are those who make money doing good, but don't trust the stock market anymore. They are looking for alternative ways to make their money grow. I'm convinced most people are looking for two things: *TIME AND MONEY.* People who tend to have a lot of time seem to not always have a lot of money. Those who have a lot of money, tend to not have much time. The question then becomes, how do you have both?

253

COREY PETERSON

I believe that real estate can help one acquire both. In fact, I believe most people reading this book want to be doing real estate in some way, shape or form. Here is the problem: most wealthy people are incredibly busy. They are usually business owners or high level corporate professionals. Because these types of people are very focused on what they do, they lack the time it takes to learn the ins and outs of the real estate market.

They really want to, but cannot seem to ever get there.

This is where my company steps in. We have spent thousands of hours mastering what we do in the real estate industry. We buy apartment complexes (in good markets) that provide cashflow and back-end profits. This is what busy professionals desire and need. We do this using a unique process which allows everyone to win in an asset class they do not build anymore.

When I talk with business owners and high net worth professionals, I tend to see a common theme. If I asked them to look at their net worth and tell me where their money is parked, the answer would surprise you. Did you know that most people's money is not parked in cash? Think about it; where is most of your savings right now? If you are like most, it's probably in your Individual Retirement Account

(IRA), or some qualified account such a 401K. Why is this? Because we have been conditioned to put our money in these vehicles. They are a great place to put money, as it can grow tax deferred and tax free if you have a Roth IRA.

Now for the mind-blowing question. Did you know you can invest in real estate using your IRA or qualified account? The answer is yes, you can.

The reason you may not know this is because most people open accounts with firms they see on TV – think Merrill Lynch, Morgan Stanley, etc. In these types of brokerages, you can only invest in what the brokerage has allowed their financial advisors to sell. Usually, this consists of all paper assets - CD's, bonds, stocks, mutual funds, etc. When you ask an advisor to invest in real estate, they will offer you a REIT, Real Estate Investment Trust. Which, by the way, is still a paper asset.

What you want is a Self-Directed IRA company that will be the fiduciary for you and allow you to invest in alternative investments, like real estate. By using your IRA money that has a longer-term outlook and making it grow with consistent returns, your wealth can grow leaps and bounds.

Let me take you on an educational journey of how I made it in real estate and how I have unlocked the secrets of creating massive cashflow for my investors by buying apartment buildings. I think you will find the stories fun and exciting! By the end of the book, you may want to get some yourself! Paradise awaits you in these chapters. Be bold, read on as I open up the play book sharing how I operate and control multi-million-dollar assets using other people's money. And, most importantly, how I help them earn a great return on their investment.

Corey Peterson

GETTING FIRED WAS MY SALVATION

I GREW UP IN A small town in Missouri that had a population of less than 18,000. In fact, that was the town. Our house was located 25 minutes out in the country. My parents, four siblings and I lived in a small two-bedroom house on a 180-acre farm.

We learned the value of hard work on that farm. We learned how to pick rock. We learned how to bale hay. More importantly, we learned the lessons that only someone raised in the country would know. You can take a country boy, put him into the city and he's fine. But bring a city kid to the country and well, it's miserable for him. Although we had a farm and we raised beef cattle, my father was a roofer by trade. He owned his own roofing business and taught me the trade. As a matter of fact, as my grandpa had taught my father that trade as well, I was in line to be a 3ʳᵈ generation roofer. What my father really taught me was I never wanted to be a roofer. The man working up on a roof was not who I knew my father to be – I did not know that guy. All I knew was, on the roof, he was the absolute boss and my job was to make sure I never made him look bad. That meant working extremely hard and doing the best job I could every single time. Although life was tough living in the country, to this day, I would not trade those lessons and gifts I learned in my youth.

For Dad's roofing lesson, it was a wise one. You see, I'm a country boy at heart. I believe in waving to others as you drive down the road. I believe you help out your fellow man in need. I believe in doing what's right. I also believe in doing what I say I'll do and speaking in plain English, without embellishment. In other words, get to the point and say what's on your mind.

In 2003, I had an incredible opportunity to go on a vacation that would ultimately change my life. My future wife and I flew to Hawaii with my mom and her husband, who had a home on the beach in

Kauai - better known as "The Garden Island." This place was absolutely amazing. The home was right on the beach. You could run out into the back yard, walk over the berm, and WHAM! You were in the soft white sand watching the powerful ocean waves crash down. It gets better though - not only was the home right on the ocean, it was located on a cove. We walked around the cove early our first morning and I was astonished at what I saw - a fresh water stream from the mountains above came rushing through and into the ocean. This place was something magical! I never could have dreamed how great this place was. This is probably why, to this day, it's my favorite vacation spot.

As I soak in the island, I look at my mom's husband, who I will call Bruce Wayne. I looked at Bruce and he didn't seem to have a care in this world. He was just there playing and enjoying life as Shelley and I were. When I took a closer look, he had nice cars in the garage, fine art in his home, and his phone was not ringing off the hook. He didn't seem to be worried about business. I knew then that I needed to ask Bruce what he did for a living. I saw he had the two things most people only dream of: time and money.

It took a while, but I was finally able to muster enough confidence to approach Bruce and ask him what he did for a living. When I asked, he simply looked at me and said, "Real Estate." Now, me being young and naïve, responded by saying, "so you're a realtor?" "No, No." Bruce said, "They work for me."

I left Hawaii and all I could think was that Bruce was indeed the BIG KAHUNA. He had time and money and lived by his own rules. I wanted that, but I just didn't know how to get it.

A year later, in 2004, I pick up a book that had been getting a lot of press and finally decided to read it. I wanted to understand what all the hype was about. The book was called "Rich Dad Poor Dad" by Robert Kiyosaki. This book changed my life forever. When I finished reading it, I knew exactly what Bruce Wayne was. He was a Real Estate Investor. I understood that he leveraged his money with bank money and bought cash flowing assets to put money into his pocket each month. I now understood why Bruce had so much time available. He set himself up to live on the cash flow from his business that bought multi-family apartments.

I now became obsessed with learning more. I would go into Barnes and Noble, peruse the Real Estate section and buy all the books I could find. I read books every day and night, seeing and learning the different strategies, strengthening my mind and crafting my plan. I knew what I wanted to do and finally in JuIy of 2005, I created my flagship company Kahuna Investments LLC. It was aptly named because I wanted to be the

BIG KAHUNA!

I loved to read, and the books I read advised calling banks and talking to the Real Estate Owned (REO) departments. I opened the yellow pages and went to Credit Unions. I felt they were not as intimidating as the "big bad: corporate banks. There I found American Airlines Federal Credit Union at the top of the list. Nervously, I dialed the number and when the receptionist answered, I squeaked out something that sounded like, "Can I talk to the head of your REO department?" I ended up speaking to a woman named Holly. Holly was the head of the REO Department and she had properties available in Tulsa, Oklahoma. The books taught me to have cash available as a down payment. So, for operating capital, I took out a home equity line of credit. I bought my first two homes from Holly. I flipped them and made some money - $15,000 on one and $20,000 on the other.

I did so well I quit my job.

However, I soon found out that was a mistake. The next three properties I bought were rentals, and this was where I ran into my first real issue. *I RAN OUT OF MONEY.* I put all the money I earned from the sale of the first two homes into my rental properties. I didn't have enough income to stay in the real estate business. Back to square one. I wanted to look for a new job that I could leverage for Real Estate. I accepted a job as a financial advisor. I knew if I did well in this position, the potential to earn a significant income was there. I could then show proof-of-income to banks in order for them to lend me money. During that process, we moved to Phoenix, Arizona. I enjoyed three years of selling securities in a great market. Then in 2008, it all changed for the worse; the market crashed. Not only did people's investments lose half their value, but in a years' time (in 2009) Phoenix real estate values dropped by half as well.

What happened next was my salvation. I had lost all desire to be a financial advisor. It seemed all the investments I made early on were in the gutter. Moreover, the people that came into my office were crying and scared to death. I really hated my job. So, when my boss scheduled a meeting with me, I knew there was a good chance I would be let go. I remember walking into the office, looking at my administrative assistant, and knowing the call had been made. She couldn't even look at me. I walked calmly into my office, sat down, and felt a moment of despair.

I couldn't believe it; I was going to get FIRED.

As my time as a financial advisor came to an end, an old desire burned back inside me. Somehow, while pursuing the game of stocks and bonds, I somehow had forgotten about real estate. As if awoken from a dream, I began to look around and saw real estate was on sale again.

It was on Sale BIG TIME....

I couldn't believe it - I had just been saved from being crushed in the real estate market by becoming a financial advisor. Shortly thereafter, I found myself on the other side with real estate prices at an all-time low.

Every book I had ever read all had a common theme. When the market is down, that is the best time to win. And win BIG in real estate. I had just been fired and was really struggling with what I should do next. Yet as I walked out of my office, I knew I couldn't just go home.

I took a short five-minute drive, arrived at Starbucks and ordered some hot coffee. It was time to figure things out. You see, I had this kid in my head that used to dream really big and wanted to win. It was that same good ol' country boy who knew he could do the hard work. He believed if he fully committed himself he could be great. But that kid was staring up at this older guy full of self-doubt. He was thinking about security, how the world worked, about supporting his family, and all the things that come along with being an adult. Suddenly, he wasn't so sure…

I was at a crossroads with myself. I knew what I wanted to do; I had known it for a very long time. I wanted to be like Bruce. I wanted time and money and freedom. I'm proud to say as I write this book, that the little kid kicked the crap out of the man and won the day.

It was in that moment that I made the most honest, noble, and courageous commitment to me. I vowed to myself that I was going to become a successful real estate investor. I made a commitment to MYSELF that I would never be defeated, and that I would never, ever quit. And although I didn't know exactly how I would get there, I left Starbucks with the resolve that I was going to make it in real estate or else. Now, all I had to do was tell my wife…

Training and Getting Started

Once I committed, I knew I needed real education. I went to a Rich Dad's Real Estate training program, a Robert Kiyosaki event. It was there that I met Bob Norton. Bob was offering a system called "KISS Flipping" – "Keep It Simple Stupid" Flipping. I invested in his course, and immediately learned he was different. Up to this point, all the books I had read taught old and out-of-date systems. By the time I was reading about their strategies, they had changed. But KISS FLIPPING was internet based, a strategy that was working. Bob became my first mentor, and showed me how to use the Multiple Listing Service (MLS) to find Real Estate Owned (REO) properties and short sales. I took that system and blew it up.

Bob offered "50/50" deals - he would provide all necessary funding, but I had to find deals and manage the rehab. If the deals met his specific criteria, he would split profits with me 50/50. Once Bob shared the outline of an acceptable 50/50 deal and showed me how to find them, I quickly became one of his top guys. At one point, we had almost $1 million "on the street." Things were going so well that Bob's brother wanted a piece of the business. However, this meant I was once again, out of a job.

Back in crisis mode, what do I do? My work with Bob had been my only source of income, I was performing well, and I enjoyed doing it. However, there was a silver lining. Bob had taught me how to lock up and control deals. He'd also taught me to take videos and pictures of every deal I ever did. I found this gave me "street cred" in the market. I took that information, created a marketing piece (with video links) and brought it to my local REIA (Real Estate Investors Association). I presented myself as a Real Estate Wholesaler and my deals where PHAT. I soon found two multi-millionaires who wanted to buy my properties. We ended up having a great working relationship.

Eventually I smartened up and raised my first piece of private capital… totally by accident.

By working the 50/50 deals with Bob and wholesaling my own deals, building my business, I had built up a solid wholesaling track record. I had finally convinced myself I knew what I was doing. I found a glitch though - I was taking small fees on the wholesale side, yet giving away the big profits to the investors. I knew my deals were good because, in fact, I tracked them even after my investors sold them. I put in a lot of work finding the deals, yet they made most of the profit. It was clear that I needed to find a way to earn the big profit and pay someone else the wholesaling fee.

I knew I didn't have a great deal of cash, yet knew that was what was required to do more real estate deals. How could I convince others to "give me their money" so I could financially help us both? And more importantly, I could pay that small fee out in interest, thus making the big money for myself. Unfortunately for me, I had no idea how to do this. I grew up with little means and although I had learned the financial markets as an advisor, I was still afraid to ask others for money. What I didn't know then, that I know now, is that I wasn't asking people for their money - I had a real opportunity to share.

I raised my first piece of private money totally by accident. I played racquetball with one of my old investors (we will call him Carl). Carl was with me in my Financial Advisor days. This gentleman had most of his money tied up in investments called annuities. While they paid him cash flow, he could not get out of them. I didn't think he had any other available extra money. But, Carl did live in a retirement community and I figured he might know some people who would be interested. I told Carl that if he knew anyone looking to make some extra money, I could pay 12% and give a house as collateral against the loan. Carl played racquetball with me every Thursday and he had watched me grow my business. But I really didn't think he had any extra money, so I was asking Carl for help as a friend. After I gave Carl my spiel, he looked at me and said, "yeah, I'll see what I can do." That was that, and we went back to playing racquetball.

The next day I got a call from… guess who…???

You guessed it, Carl. He said, "Corey, do you still want to do that deal and pay 12%?" I replied, "Sure." I was so thrilled - Carl had found someone who was interested. I was "doing the happy dance." Then Carl proceeded to tell me, "Corey, I'm not sure if you know this, but my home is totally paid for. And if you are willing to pay 12% for money, I can borrow against my house at 3.2%. That means I can make a spread. Corey, how much money do you need?"

To that I replied, "Carl, I need $85,000 for the deal." Carl simply said, "Great. Where do you want me to send it?"

This question caught me off guard. You should understand, at this point,

I hadn't made the necessary arrangements to see the deal all the way through. I fumbled for a minute and let Carl know I'd have to get back with him. A couple days later, I made arrangements with my title company for Carl to wire his money to them. This marked a milestone in my career - my first deal with OPM "Other People's Money."

When this happened, all I can tell you is, I felt like Clark Kent running down the alley pulling his suit out to reveal Superman. I had never dreamed of other people giving me their money. I was humbled that someone trusted me enough to make their money grow. It was an awesome feeling!

The Money is in the Money

I learned to perfect the capital raising business, and a very valuable lesson. I thought that real estate was "where it's at" and in a way, it was. What I have come to realize is, the money is not in real estate - the money is in the money. You can find all the deals you want, but without any money to buy them, you will always settle for that smaller paycheck. Once I found this to be true, I began to seek out mentors who were raising lots of capital.

I needed a guide for taking people's money. I created a "private money program guide" with the purpose of educating investors on how my company worked and how we invested people's money. To get a copy of my guide, go to **www.WhyTheRich-GetRicher.net/downloads.** I taught my investors how to play the bank and lend my company money to do deals. Another piece I created was my Credibility Kit. Using all the videos and pictures in my portfolio, I compiled all my previous wholesale and rehab deals. I then created a document detailing my expertise. In other words, I could now tell a story about how I used other people's money to buy real estate, and more importantly make it grow. It didn't take long before I realized I needed to be in a leadership role. With leadership in mind, I created an REIA (Real Estate Investor Association) called "East Valley Investors Club" - which still exists today. I teach others what I do in my wholesale single family business. This, in turn, helps me with credibility and notoriety, which helps to raise more private money. People with money want to do business with other successful people. It didn't take long before I had millions of dollars on the street working, doing flips and rehabs.

Shifting Gears

My business flipping single family homes was going nicely. I had lots of private money lined up and I was able to find deals using the MLS. That was until the market began to change. You see for me, I had only learned one way to find deals. Remember how Bob Norton taught me to find deals on the MLS with REOs and short sales? He'd never taught me the art of marketing. So, when the short sales and REO became harder and harder to find, it was like "Houston, we have a problem." It became clear I needed to find another way to source single family homes, and do so quickly. Yet, I had something a little bigger in mind. I knew my private investors were counting on me to be able to place their investments and make their money grow. I had a hunch my next idea would be awesome.

Big Deals Big Money

When I first started investing in 2005, I vividly remember driving by apartment complexes and saying to myself, "I wish I could own one of those." Really, at that point in my life, wishing meant "it's a pipe dream." But here I was in a market where I had lots of private money behind me and was driving by apartments saying the same darn thing. I wish... I wish...I wish...

But things changed the day I reframed my mindset and hit the reset button in my brain. Instead of *wishing* I could buy an apartment complex, I asked myself a simple question: "How *could* I buy an apartment complex?" By framing it as a question, all the power in my brain started firing. The next question to myself was, "Corey, what do you know about apartments or multi-family buildings?" I answered truthfully and said, "not much." I asked myself another question, "Where could you get some information on multi-family apartments?" Once again, without hesitation, my brain gave me the answer: Go to the bookstore and see what's out there.

Next thing I knew, I purchased seven books from, you guessed it, AMAZON, and started to take in all the information I could. I was looking for an author I could relate to and help me understand the process. Unfortunately, it took me until book #7, the last book I read, to hit the jackpot. The book I'm referring to? "Multi-Family Millions," by Dave Lindahl. Dave owned more than 7,000 units and had a lot of knowledge. More importantly, Dave wrote in such a way that I could understand exactly what he was doing. I knew I needed to meet him.

While I wanted to invest in his course, I made it clear I wouldn't make the purchase unless I was able to personally have lunch with Dave. I wanted to do my due diligence.

It's important to do so and not be influenced by a flashy presentation or one 30-minute speech.

So, I flew to Boston, where Dave lives, from my home in Phoenix just to have lunch and get to know him as a person. He's honest, hardworking, came from nothing like I did, and his family works in his business. He's a stand-up guy, has taught me the ropes, and has been a true mentor. We recently did an interview discussing the value of mentorship. To see this interview, go to **www.WhyTheRichGetRicher.net/DavidLindahl.**

Dave taught me how to underwrite, locate and find cash flowing deals.

More than that, he showed me how to properly structure the deals.

After doing countless underwritings on potential apartment deals, I felt it was finally time to actually bring one in. I still had the huge problem of millions of dollars in private monies that needed to be placed, yet no single-family deals to put it in. I knew it was only a matter of time before I found a deal that made sense. And wouldn't you know it, a deal fell in my lap. Well, not actually - here's what happened and how I did my first apartment deal.

After lots of searching and talking with many brokers in areas in which I wanted to invest, I was getting a decent amount of deals to look at and underwrite. I just hadn't found the perfect one. Since this was to be my first shot out of the gate, I knew I needed a deal with a lot of "meat on the bone." But how I found my first deal surprised even me.

By now, I was an avid fan of Dave Lindahl's and I had been taking all of his courses. I attended his 'Manage the Manager' event in Rhode Island. Upon arrival, I told myself I was going to do things differently. Instead of being busy, trying to network and find other like-minded people, I specifically wanted to see if I could catch a deal. So, when the opportunity presented itself, I stood up tall and from the back of the room, I belted out, "My name is Corey Peterson with Kahuna Investments. I have a crap ton of cash and I'm looking for deals." By the end of the weekend, I was able to see every deal other investors had. I had managed to flip the script and didn't even mean to. I now had investors chasing me, wanting me to give them money.

On a quick side note, I'm going to repeat something. *The Money is in the Money.* Remember this… the money is always patient, never acts in haste, is always prudent and always demands the best possible outcome. He who has the money, makes the rules.

As I stated, I looked at many deals that weekend. But one deal, in particular, really stood out. It was a 144-unit deal in Greenville, South Carolina called Lionsgate. The price tag on this property was $3.2 million. I really liked the economics of the Carolinas and felt this property had all the right things wrong.

It was an REO that suffered from bad personnel and management, as well as a lot of deferred maintenance. Deferred maintenance is a nice way of saying the current owner let things go downhill and didn't upkeep the property. These issues were all very fixable and I knew it could be done quickly. Even better, the group that had the deal under contract was in a pickle. They had $100,000 hard - meaning if they did not close, they would lose the money. Not only was their money hard, the group only had 15 days to close. The amount of money needed to fully fund the deal was around $1.4 million. Not only was I able to negotiate a 75% ownership stake in the deal, I also brought in all the money for it as well. I eventually bought out the investors and now own it 100%. But it gets better. As I write this book, we just listed Lionsgate on the market for $9 million. Pretty cool, right?

Once I learned the formula, I simply repeated the process over and over again. Find deals, fund them and operate the properties for cash flow. It's a fairly simple process, but it takes a great team to properly execute it. And fortunately for my company, we have the best team out there.

PERFECTING THE PROCESS

THIS BOOK IS FOR the 40+ year old individual or business level executive who earns a considerably high income and wants their money to work as hard as they do. One of today's financial problems is that few people truly understand the stock market. At times, it goes up and down for what appears to be no reason. What I have come to find out is most investors hate the volatility of the stock market. I've also found that many investors have most of their money in qualified accounts like IRA and Roth IRA, leading them to believe their only investment options are stocks, bonds and mutual funds. Basically, whatever their broker offers and suggests – paper assets. Most people are not aware they can use their IRA money to invest in real estate. When we show people how, it blows their minds.

Remember, people don't trust the stock market. Furthermore, they realize what will happen once the Baby Boomers begin to cash in their retirement funds and start drawing them down. Suddenly, there's going to be a tremendous demand for liquid cash, which will really hurt the stock market.

What I love about our business model is that our investors become owners with us in the deal. More importantly, they can visit and touch the building. It's not pie in the sky. Most people who are savvy investors know they should have some real estate in their portfolio. We allow a shortcut to the source.

With that said, many of our new investors have been referrals from past clients who are happy with what we've done for them. It's not uncommon for someone to call me and say he's interested in finding out about the opportunities we offer.

When this happens, the first thing I like to do is to find out what kind of investor they are and what they want to achieve. I've learned over the years that you must listen.

I've seen people get pushed into deals that may not have been what they're looking for. Situations such as this can be alleviated by having a simple conversation. You need to know people's risk tolerance. Have they done any prior real estate deals? What's the investor's time horizon? Can they stay in a deal for up to 5 years? Are they seeking yield or are they seeking cash flow? I think most people want a little of both. Most investors want to make a solid return that pays cash flow and provides a chance to make a little more upside. I have found that almost everyone loves mailbox money, and loves the idea of getting checks every quarter.

As I have great conversations with potential investors, I'm also thinking to myself "do I want this person in my deal?" There's nothing worse than having a five-year professional relationship with someone you simply do not get along with or is the proverbial thorn in your side.

I've also come to realize that Kahuna is not always the right fit for everybody. Sometimes it's easier to tell people "no" in the beginning, before we get too far along in the process. It saves everybody a lot of time, headaches, trials and tribulations. I've had some investors with large amounts of money to spend that expect huge returns. They've been conditioned to take on very risky deals and are chasing a huge yield. We're just not that shop.

What we try to achieve in our deals is the consistency factor. We base them on the criteria that people have a basic need for food, clothing and shelter. We like to do what I call the "shelter mission." Our approach is to be very systematic and straightforward. We like to find a "working man's" type of apartment complex. These apartments were built between 1970 and the early 1990's. They don't have flashy amenities the new complexes have, but they do service a large portion of the population. I believe that people, regardless of income, will always gravitate to the best possible housing within their budget. Our goal is to make the apartments we operate the best in their class, pulling the best tenants in that particular price range. People want clean, affordable living. If we can deliver that, and shorten someone's commute, that's a recipe for success. That's our objective.

The first call with a potential client is a preliminary conversation to see if we are a good fit for one another. In the current market, there are many more people seeking this type of investment than there are good, safe, solid investments. We want to make sure that personality-wise, the person is a good fit with us.

The next step is to look at their current position - not just financially, but physically and emotionally. We want to ensure that, not only is the investment a good fit for their current portfolio, and the risk tolerance is right, but their expectations are reasonable and achievable.

Finally, we want to know if the investor is educated and accredited who is hands-on, or will they need significant education before we proceed?

Once we know the investor's basic status, and they have filled out our Accredited Investors Form*, we then send out our Credibility Kit. Remember I had one for my single-family flips? I also have one for my multi-family business.

> *indicates they have a net worth of $1 million or more (not including their personal home) or earn an annual income of at least $250K a year.

The Kahuna Credibility Kit outlines the type of properties we target - which sizes and locations. It contains information about our process, as well as our team. It also shows a potential investor what we own and operate. Our goal is to make sure we can show you, without a doubt, that we are indeed experts at what we do. I've spent over 1,000 hours getting my education in the business and feel I've mastered the game. Let me be clear, though. I've mastered single-family flips, single-family wholesale and multi-family apartments. In those areas,

I'm very skilled and knowledgeable. Yet, if you asked me to take on a commercial office or retail space, I would tell you "I'm not your man." What I've learned over time is that experts make money. In the areas I've just shared, I'm that expert. I've also learned the generalist usually makes excuses, and that's the reason why I won't engage in business deals other than those within my core competencies.

Not only will I send out our Credibility Kit, but if we are in the process of working a deal, I will send details on it as well. We call this our Property Packet - a brochure explaining our investment and how it works. Of course, there are times we're not going to have deals working. Our goal then is to have enough people raising their hands saying they "want in" on our upcoming deal. Since our model focuses on quality deals, we may only do 3-4 deals each year.

These apartments are typically 100+ units and are big projects. Most of the time, the deals we buy require large amounts of capital in order to improve the property. To ensure we are not stressing our systems, we operate at somewhat of a slower pace. We function at this rate because if we moved much faster, we would be sacrificing quality control. When you're dealing with other people's money, it's just not worth it.

Our goal is to make sure our management team can get into the property. It is vital for us to do our due diligence on the front end, so we know what we need to move forward. This is important as we work to get our management team set up and ready to properly make moves to our property before we even start.

Another reason we choose to only do 3-4 projects a year is because it helps us, from an operational standpoint, function more efficiently. We don't want to begin a new project until we've got proper stabilization in place for existing projects. This encompasses personnel, as an integral part of the entire process. We are able to get the property moving in the right direction, toward achieving our desired goal. When we take over a new property, it's a bit like having a baby. We may be working long hours checking off to-do list items, as well as repairing many deferred maintenance projects. Once we know the property is on the right track, it's then time for us to find another.

Another reason we don't scale up too much is because my wife and I are typically the biggest investors in any of our deals. We are personally invested in making sure every deal is successful. Not only is our money in play, of course, other people's money is as well. I personally feel other people's money is more important than my own, and therefore we choose to put our investors ahead of ourselves. I don't think everybody does this, but I think they should.

The proverbial "golden goose" in what Kahuna does with apartments is raising capital. By far, this is the most important part of our operation. Our priority lies in taking care of what we call "the money" - the people who bring us their capital. Number one – we are the guardians of their money. Number two - a grower of their money.

Our investors usually get a preferred return based upon the cash flow of our deal. This means, they get first dip out of the bucket. We don't pay ourselves until our investors make that preferred return.

The fact that our investors bring us referrals proves we are doing things the right way. In fact, most of our new capital comes from referrals in the networks of people currently invested in our deals. Additionally, most current investors usually want to be included in our next ones. They love the experience and begin to see for themselves how it really works for them. They like seeing the mailbox money! Who wouldn't? If you want to learn how you can earn some mailbox money for yourself, go to **www.WhyTheRichGetRicher.net/Income** to let us know you're interested. We will send you our Credibility Kit and start the process. Accredited investors only, please.

Doing Due Diligence

Once we have a deal in place and have qualified our investor, we then send out our Property Packet. At this point, we typically have the property under contract and a minimum of $100,000 in earnest money secured. Remember, the Property Packet lays out the foundation of how we foresee the deal going, as well as how we need to operate in order to increase value. It also includes a 5-year conservative underwriting projection. This takes into account our experience in operations, as well as shows our estimated investor returns.

When we lock a property in contract, there's usually a period of time allowed for inspections. This is the "due diligence" period. It's the time we take to review the property's total condition. There are two stages: physical due diligence and financial due diligence. During physical due diligence, we do things like check electric and A/C systems, plumbing, overall condition of each unit, the outside of the building, as well as a roof inspection. We then obtain estimates for any work that may need to be done. This is all done before we make a purchase decision so as to ensure we will meet our targeted rehab budgets. To ensure a comprehensive overview of the property, we use a combination of licensed inspectors and a head maintenance supervisor. After the physical stage, we then start financial due diligence. Although I'm referring to these as two separate stages, we normally have two teams working simultaneously.

In the financial due diligence stage, we look at and verify all property numbers. We look at each tenant and review their lease jacket. Kahuna closely examines each tenant's credit score, payment history and crime record. In addition, we identify tenants who may no longer meet our criteria. When these leases are up for renewal, Kahuna reserves the right to deny. The next step is to review utility expenditures such as electricity, water, sewer and waste. We look specifically at historical figures to ensure they match the seller provided financials. Our job is to know where all money comes from and goes to. We also search for expenses that can be eliminated. You'd be surprised how many apartment owners are overpaying for the same items we get for much less. This inspection process is typically a $10,000 expense. I will tell you, it's worth every penny. In this business, you do NOT want surprises. It's always better to measure twice and only cut once.

In our packet, we provide several useful pieces of information – unit quantity, unit mix (one bedroom, two, etc.), and where we see opportunity. Also, and I think more importantly, we provide what we view as the economic situation of not only the property, but the city in which the property is located. We need to ensure we will be operating in a city large enough to make sense. We look for indicators, such as a local airport with major carriers, universities/colleges, large hospitals, and a strong job market. Surprisingly, we try to stay away from major markets. We prefer submarkets and usually find better opportunities. As far as economic indicators, we look for a growing work force. This means jobs are coming into the area, not leaving. This is very important.

As we consider an area, we also look at crime statistics. Typically, women are the decision makers when it comes to where their families live. Selecting areas with low crime rates is very important to them. The Kahuna threshold is a crime rate below both the state average and within the property's zip code. Another factor we take into consideration is the traffic count from the nearest major streets and thruways. It's important to know how many people regularly drive those roads. After all, they are future prospects.

It all circles back to our main idea: when we can provide affordable, clean housing, and shorten someone's commute, we win every time. In short, we do our due diligence and that's how we anticipate maintaining occupancy in our properties.

At this point in the process, our investors have a property packet in hand, and they have reviewed the deal and more than likely have many questions. They want to understand our plan to create value. How will we increase rent? How will we repair and update the property making it clean and nice, yet still maximize profitability? That's usually done in a one-on-one discussion. We prefer face-to-face, but many of our investors are out of state, so we defer to technology by using a webinar format. This ensures both parties are looking at the same thing and are actively learning about the deal.

When we send a property packet to a potential investor, we usually already have a fairly accurate picture of what improvements need to be completed. But sometimes, we miss things. For this reason, once we are officially under contract, we spend approximately $10,000 on a formal inspection. We closely examine the health of the entire property, both physical and financial.

For one property in particular, it was raining the day we were on site. We saw eight active leaks. The seller had to have known about these leaks; however, they were never disclosed. Since we had hired a skilled roofer to inspect properties, we found the leaks. This left us with decisions to make. It's not uncommon for sellers not to disclose things. We see it often and therefore we rely on our process. A complete roof replacement on that project would essentially kill the deal. Luckily for us, we had a plan.

Knowing we had roof leaks, our team secured multiple bids and told the seller, regardless if we purchased his property or not, it would be in his best interests to repair the problem. We received multiple bids and could show, beyond a doubt, we could not incur the cost of a repair deferment. Our due diligence allowed us to obtain a $175,000 roof. With that credit, we could still make our numbers work and knew our property would soon have a brand-new roof. If we hadn't secured that credit, the deal would more than likely have dissolved. At that point, it was just not workable; our numbers would tell us so. Remember, we were unaware of the roof problem and therefore hadn't budgeted for it. The actual cost of replacing the roof was $225,000, so the $175,000 went a very long way. Without the seller credit, our numbers would not have allowed for us to incur the cost risk of installing a new roof. Sometimes we plan on doing deals, but when things go wrong, we have learned through experience to not force it. That's how you get into trouble. We have learned to trust our process and not waver from it.

Once we finish Due Diligence (inspection period), and have negotiated with the seller for anything we were unhappy with, it is at that point we go hard. Hard means our earnest money is now at risk and we need to close. Finally, we are ready to create our Private Placement Memorandum - a document used to pool capital together and begin to work with our investors to fund the deal. This document reviews the property and its operation in detail, and is regulated by the Security and Exchange Commission. It's prepared by a lawyer and costs between $15,000 to $20,000 to prepare. When we are running the property, the PPM and its rules are what guide us when it comes to distributions, payments, etc.

Once we have received the money, we set the closing date. Next, we close on the property and the real work begins!! Operations – this is where most investors fail. Unfortunately, they do not understand the complexity of projects nor do they have the necessary knowledge. We also have a few special tricks we implement in our units. I'll talk about them in a later chapter. Just know I'm going to reveal some Wudan Shaolin Monk Kung Fu in the way my team operates. It's truly first class.

The only real question is, do you want to learn more about being one of our investors in our deals?

To get your **FREE** copy of
Why the Rich Get Richer, vist
www.whytherichgetricher.com

About the Author

As the owner of Kahuna Investments, Corey strives to provide his investors with stable cash flow returns and long-term capital appreciation by buying multi-family apartments. Corey has managed and acquired over $95million in real estate across the country. He is the bestselling author of "Why The Rich Get Richer –The Secrets to Cash-Flowing Apartments" and host of the Multi-Family Legacy Podcast. He speaks around the country on this subject, including at Harvard and Nasdaq. Corey is frequently featured on FOX, CBS, ABC, and NBC affiliates.

Business is not everything. Corey serves as a member of Rotary International, and has hosted several foreign exchange students at his home. Furthermore, Corey donates his time to Junior Achievement, where he teaches high school students. In a 10-week program, these young people learn entrepreneurial skills and focus on creating a business and developing products to bring to market.

To learn more about how Corey can help you get massive cashflow by buying apartment buildings, contact him directly at admin@kahunainvestments.com, or visit his website to learn more about his services at **www.KahunaWealthBuilders.com.**